WOMEN OF THE BIBLE TELL THEIR STORIES

MARY E. JENSEN

AUGSBURG Publishing House • Minneapolis

WOMEN OF THE BIBLE TELL THEIR STORIES

Copyright © 1978 Augsburg Publishing House

Library of Congress Catalog Card No. 78-52193

International Standard Book No. 0-8066-1663-6

Scripture quotations are from the Revised Standard Version of the Bible, copyright 1946, 1952, and 1971 by the Division of Christian Education of the National Council of Churches.

MANUFACTURED IN THE UNITED STATES OF AMERICA

To my mother-in-law, Carrie H. Jensen,
and to the memory of
my mother, Mari O. Halvorson,
who have exemplified to me
strong, victorious Christian womanhood

Contents

Introduction

In the Scriptures we are afforded glimpses into the lives of many women. It soon becomes apparent that their decisions and actions were important in the course of not only human history but also salvation history.

Sometimes we have a tendency to canonize people of the Bible, feeling that they were somehow more holy or saintly than we can possibly be today. "Our situation is very different," we say. It's true that our culture and environment are different from theirs. Sarah did not ride in an automobile on her long journey, nor did Lydia have a computerized cash register in her place of business. But the essential things about life are the same: people face sickness, despair, and death; they experience joy and happiness; they need strong, loving relationships with other people; they crave a right relationship with God.

The 20 dramas in this book bring to life brief moments from the Bible as seen through the eyes and the experiences of women. The women are acquainted with life and death, birth and child rearing, careers and callings, joys and fears, just as we are. As we learn about their lives and experiences, we can gain insights into our own lives and relationships with God. As we probe their thoughts and responses to their situations, we find ourselves looking in a mirror. Hannah gave her precious son, Samuel, to God. How do I turn my children over to God? Mary Magdalene followed Jesus right to the cross and the tomb. What does faithful discipleship to Christ mean in my life?

Drama is a powerful educational tool. The realism of a dramatic moment can take our breath away, suddenly peeling back centuries of time. For a moment we see and hear Pilate's wife as she agonizes over the trial of Jesus. For an instant we experience Mary's grief as she watches her son die on the cross. But the power of drama comes not only in the momentary experience, but also in the ongoing remembrance and application of God's Word to our lives.

The medium is drama. The message is response to God. The result is heightened awareness of Scriptures and our own relationship and response to God.

Use of the dramas

The 20 dramas presented in this book are monologs. One woman acts out the experiences and thoughts of a particular biblical woman. The only exception to this is the drama *Mary and Martha* in which two women present their thoughts. Each gives a monolog, but in the same drama.

These dramatic monologs are designed to teach, entertain, and inspire. Drama is as old as the human race. It has been used to teach the Scriptures for many centuries. Passion and miracle plays were presented in medieval churches. The word "marionette" means "little Mary." Like our forebears, we can use drama to create special moments, and then use the special moments to teach and inspire people with the good news that God was and is active in human history.

The scriptural basis appears at the beginning of each monolog. I have used my imagination to elaborate on the stories told in the Scriptures. Occasionally sentences in quotation marks are direct quotations from the Revised Standard Version of the Bible, but frequently I have written the words, either paraphrasing the Scriptures or adding dialog as it might have occurred.

To enable readers to easily find particular dramas, the book is divided into four sections: Old Testament, Christmas, Easter, and New Testament.

The dramas are organized within each section according to sequence of occurrence. For instance, in the Christmas section we hear from Ruth, who is a forebear of Christ; then from Mary, who has been visited by the angel to announce the conception of Jesus; then from the imaginary innkeeper's wife, who tells about the birth in the stable; and then from Anna, the old prophetess who saw Jesus as an infant in the temple and proclaimed him as God's salvation.

There are many possible uses for the dramas:

Worship services   A particular drama may fit with scripture readings any time during the church year. The drama can be used in place of the sermon, to lead into the sermon, or to amplify the text.

Seasonal services or programs   The Christmas and Easter dramas may be used at regular services or at special services during these seasons of the church year. One or more of the dramas could be used at Christmas concerts and church school programs or Easter services. For instance, the humorous innkeeper's wife tells the Christmas story in a rustic yet strikingly beautiful way. The drama of Mary at the foot of the cross is a stunning addition to a Good Friday service, while the drama of Mary Magdalene is exceptionally well-suited to an Easter sunrise service. The drama *Mary, Mother of Jesus (III)* would be appropriate for Pentecost.

A combination of two or three dramas often makes a good program. Use your imagination to create unusual groupings of dramas appropriate to the needs of the church year or the program theme. For example:

• The three dramas of Mary, the mother of Jesus, may be used in order, with appropriate music between the dramas, and devotional application before and after presentation.

• The dramas of Dorcas, Lydia, and Priscilla depict the growth of the early Christian church.

• An emphasis on motherhood is found in the dramas about Ruth, Sarah, and the Shunammite woman.

• An emphasis on worship and prayer is found in the dramas about Hannah, the Shunammite woman, and Anna.

• Queen Esther, Deborah, and Lydia are women who had specific callings or careers.

• Mary Magdalene, the Shunammite woman, Mary and Martha, and Dorcas all speak of healing in their lives.

Consider the emphasis and theme of the service or program, then examine the dramas with particular needs in mind. Many combinations of two, three, or four dramas can highlight the emphasis or theme.

Women's meetings   Any of the dramas may be incorporated into programs for women, whether at monthly meetings or at large conventions. Dramas can be chosen for their appropriateness to the church year or to the theme of the meeting. For instance, the dramas about Hannah and the Shunammite woman involve prayer, the drama about Deborah depicts the use of one's talents, and Zacchaeus' wife speaks specifically to the personal acceptance of Christ.

Banquets and family nights   Drama knows no

boundaries of age or gender. Young children are captivated by the experience of seeing and hearing Queen Esther or the wife of the little man, Zacchaeus! Dramas appropriate to the church season or program theme can be presented at mother-daughter banquets and family nights.

Educational purposes   The dramas can be tape recorded and listened to during confirmation lessons or church school classes. The recorded dramas can also be used for puppet programs. In addition, teenage girls may find presenting the dramas to be an exciting educational experience. Vacation church school settings often call for dramatic presentations.

For personal reading   The dramas are conducive to personal enjoyment and devotional reading. They may also be read aloud in Bible study groups or in drama or reading clubs.

Costumes, properties, staging

Long, simple flowing gowns will greatly enhance the drama's effectiveness. At the beginning of each drama brief costume suggestions are made. However, the actress may simply wear street clothes.

Each drama may be given without any properties, either by simply reading the drama or by having the actress pantomime use of any necessary props. Suggestions for properties are given at the beginning of each drama for those who wish to use them. Properties should be simple, as is appropriate for Bible times. Wooden tables, stools, and benches work well.

The dramas can be enacted in the chancel of the

church, on a stage, or simply in front of a group of people. If a microphone is necessary, a traveling throat microphone is preferred so that movement is possible.

Reading, memorization, acting

The dramas are most effective when performed by women in costume who have memorized the lines and have thought about their movements within the scene of the dramas.

If memorization is not possible, the actress may simply read the drama after becoming familiar with the lines. The pronunciation guide at the beginning of each drama should be studied carefully.

Directions for physical motion and for emotional portrayal are found at the beginning of each drama as well as throughout the text. Instructions for use of the voice are also given.

In the drama, a series of dots between words indicates a pause or a hesitation. Such pauses add realism to the dramas, since we do not, in ordinary conversation, use long, complete sentences. We often pause . . . to collect our thoughts!

Women presenting the monologs should be approximately the age of the women portrayed, and they should be able to read or act well. A variety of actresses to present various characters is effective, although a skillful actress can change not only her costume and makeup, but also her bearing, voice, and attitude, to create several characters.

Sarah

GENESIS 15:1-6; 16; 17:15-21; 18:1-15; 21; 22

Moriah—muh-RYE-ah
Isaac—EYE-zek
Hagar—HAY-gar
Ishmael—ISH-maa-el

Sarah is an old woman, but she retains her
strength and vigor. She moves quickly and easily,
occasionally sitting on a bench in the middle of the
scene. She is dressed in a long, elegant red robe,
reflecting the fact that Abraham is a wealthy
nomad. The time is noon.

*(Sarah is wandering back and forth in the scene,
waiting and looking for someone to come. She is anxious.)*

Seven days—it's been seven days since they left!
Abraham said he was going to the land of Moriah to
sacrifice to our God. He thought it would take about
three days to journey there. If I go by that, Abraham
should have been back home yesterday. . . . But it's
already noon on the seventh day, and he's still not

14

back. Oh, my worst fears might be coming true! Maybe Abraham is afraid to come back because . . . because. . . . *(Takes a deep breath, trying to control herself.)*

Now that's silly! You really are talking like a fearful old woman, Sarah! Of *course* Abraham will come back, even if the very worst has happened. *(Paces across scene, holding both hands to her mouth, distressed, holding back tears.)*

How I wish I had never heard Abraham praying that day! I wish I had never come back to the tent! Then I wouldn't know anything about his plans. . . . I hoped and hoped that Abraham would talk to me about the journey. I tried to give him many opportunities to confide in me, but he just talked about making this trip to Moriah and sacrificing to our God. I asked why he wasn't taking a sacrificial lamb the way he always has before. He just said that the trip was God's command and that God would provide the sacrificial lamb. And Abraham insisted that Isaac go along on the journey. Why, Isaac has never been away from me or from his home for this length of time! He's only eight years old—why should he make this long trip to Moriah to sacrifice to our God unless . . . unless. . . . *(Cannot say the words. Struggles to control herself emotionally.)*

The trouble is—I know a lot more about this journey than I want to know. My husband thought I was at the well drawing water as he prayed in our tent. But I had forgotten one of the water pots. As I neared the tent, I heard him praying. I could not *believe* what I was hearing! My husband was praying about the trip and about the sacrifice. He was asking our God about the sacrificial lamb. And then he said, "Isaac? Isaac, my only true son?" I was horrified! I couldn't move! And inside the tent I heard Abraham sigh deeply as though he, too, was having trouble believing our God. And then I heard Abraham's words: "I believe and trust you, my God. I will take Isaac." *(Sits down on bench and rocks back and forth as she speaks.)*

My son Isaac is a miracle baby. I had been barren, childless, all my life. Suddenly, when Abraham was 100 years old and I was 90—I bore a child! Oh, Abraham had said for *years* that our God had promised that he, Abraham, would become a great nation, but I always had trouble believing it. If I couldn't bear children, then how could my husband legitimately be the father of many people? *(Gets up from bench and moves to one side of the scene.)*

Then I thought I saw a way. I was so eager for Abraham to have his son that I told him to take my maid, Hagar, as a substitute wife. I hoped Hagar could bear a child because that meant that *I,* as Abraham's legal wife, could claim the child as my own. I had come to believe that this was the only way I could ever have a child. Abraham was not pleased with this arrangement, but he finally agreed. The result was a son. . . . *(Breaks off her sentence, again looking anxiously into distance.)*

It's becoming afternoon and they're still not here. . . . I just can't forget that Abraham failed to take a sacrificial lamb on his journey. He didn't bring a lamb. . . .

He just brought . . . Isaac. *(Struggles to control herself. Takes a deep breath and seats herself on the bench, trying to think of something else.)*

Hagar's son Ishmael—at first I loved him dearly. Such a darling baby! But Hagar's attitude toward me began to change once the baby was born. She knew perfectly well that I, as Abraham's wife, was unable to bear children, and now *she,* the maid, had borne him a son. She became hateful, looking sideways at me with little smiles of contempt. I punished her, of course, but it didn't do any good. That woman still knew that *her* son, the one *she* had borne, was Abraham's only child. And Abraham loved that boy. He would play with him, tossing him in the air, listening to his baby laugh. *(Stands, straining to look into distance.)*

The rays of the sun are beginning to cast long shadows. And *still* they're not here. *(Takes a deep breath, lets it out in a rush.)* Would Abraham really sacrifice his own son? *There*—I finally said it! I've been thinking it but I have been afraid to say it. . . . I know there are religions around us that require people to sacrifice their children to their gods, but I never thought *our* God would require such a sacrifice. . . . It's not possible. It *can't* be—not after all this time! *(Moves about scene, shaking head in disbelief, then starts remembering again.)*

There was a time, shortly before I became pregnant, when Abraham had visitors. Three men came to our tent at noontime and Abraham offered them rest and refreshment. Strange—they told Abraham that I would bear a son in about a year. Oh, I couldn't help it! I laughed and laughed to myself inside the tent. This old story about me having a baby—here it was again!—this time on the lips of these three strangers.

I didn't think they could hear me laugh inside the tent, but they did. I became afraid, not knowing who they were, and I denied that I had laughed, but somehow they knew that I had. I laughed because it was *funny*—how could a husband and wife the age of Abraham and myself have a child? People just aren't *made* to have children when they reach our age! And I also laughed because it was such a sore point with me. After all the years of childlessness and all the years of enduring Hagar's malice, I could only laugh in despair.

Ishmael was 13 years old when the miracle happened. I, Sarah, at the age of 89 years, became pregnant! Who could believe such a thing?! All those years of enduring Hagar's smirks and smiles, all those years of listening to Abraham's questions and prayers, all those years of watching my friends and relatives bear child after child after child. . . . And suddenly *I'm* the one with the swelling belly and the sickness in the morning! Suddenly *I* can feel a little one kicking and poking inside me! It was incredible!

When our son was born we named him Isaac, which means "Let God laugh"—in other words, "Let our God look with affection upon this child." I remember saying, "God has made laughter for me; everyone who hears will laugh over me." I meant that everyone would be happy for me, and they were! What a beautiful, beautiful baby Isaac was. Abraham loved him so much, and I hovered over him as if he would disappear if I didn't watch him every minute!

Ishmael? Well, I had endured all of Hagar's smiles and remarks for nearly 15 years, but when I saw Ishmael and Isaac playing together, something snapped inside me. I begged Abraham to get rid of that slave woman and her son. Finally Abraham agreed and he took Hagar and Ishmael out in the desert. He gave them bread and water and left them there. Abraham didn't really want to do that, but later he told me that our God had promised to care for the woman and her child. And finally it was just Abraham, Isaac, and me in our tent. What blessings God has poured upon us! *(Looks again into distance, then looks back, her shoulders slumping.)*

But maybe I'll never see that beautiful child again. . . . Maybe Abraham really *did* sacrifice him to our God. Abraham is totally obedient to God, and if God asked Abraham for the return of his son, I think my husband would give it. . . . *(Cries out to God in despairing voice.)* Oh, my God—if you have taken Isaac, then take me, too! I cannot live without my child! *(Weeps, then suddenly comes to listening stance. Her body freezes.)* What's that? . . . What's that I hear? *(Looks all around, again peering into the distance.)*

Isaac? *(Her voice resounds with fear, and yet with hope.)* Isaac, my darling, is it *your* voice I hear? . . . Oh, it is, it *is!* Now I can *see* you coming to me! . . . *(Weeps as she watches Isaac approach.)* You've come home to me! Ohhh, I'll never let you go away again!

19

(Sees Abraham coming into the scene.) My husband! *(Reaches out to him.)* How I have waited! I wondered if . . . and I thought. . . . *(Listens to Abraham, showing wonder and surprise and joy in succession.)*

But that's wonderful, Abraham! To think that God provided the sacrifice of a ram at the very last moment! Perhaps our God was testing your faith, Abraham. And you didn't withhold your special son Isaac. I think God must have been very pleased!

Yes. . . yes, Isaac, you wash yourself now. Your father is also coming to wash after that long, long trip.

(Alone in the scene, she's relieved and joyous.) Abraham said that after the ram had been sacrificed, our God renewed his promises to him: "Because you have obeyed me, Abraham, your descendants will be as many as the stars in the sky, as many as the grains of sand on the seashore." Imagine that! *(Looks up into sky.)*

It's nearly dark now, and I can see that one bright star that comes out every night. . . . That star is like you, Isaac. At first I can only see that star, and then after a while I can see another, then another, until the sky is peppered with twinkling stars! Yes, our God is faithful. He will keep his promises!

(Laughs.) Oh, yes! *(Exits.)*

Deborah

JUDGES 4—5

Canaanite—KAY-nuh-night
Sisera—SIS-ur-ah
Megiddo—meh-GID-doe
Taanach—TAY-uh-nock
Deborah—DEB-uh-rah
Ramah—RAY-muh
Lappidoth—LAP-ih-doth
Ephraim—EE-frah-im
Manasseh—muh-NAS-uh
Issachar—IZ-zah-car
Zebulun—ZEB-you-lun
Naphtali—NAF-tuh-lye

Reuben—ROO-ben
Jabin—JAY-bin
Canaan—KAY-nun
Barak—BEAR-ak
Kedesh—KEH-desh
Kishon—KIH-shon
Tabor—TAY-bore
Jezreel—jez-REEL
Heber—HEE-bur
Kenite—KEE-night
Jael—JAY-uhl

Deborah moves with assurance and with the
wisdom of experience. She may be an older woman
with the grace of movement which age can bring.
She is tired, and her movements reflect that.

A bench should be provided for her to sit on.
She wears a long, flowing robe, perhaps one with
bright-colored stripes. She may wear a scarf tied
like a turban around her head, or perhaps a long
scarf lightly draped around her head or shoulders.

Oh, Barak, you keep singing with the people if you want to! I must get a drink of cool water and rest for a while. *(Walks to imaginary well and draws water, then sits on bench. Drinks water, savoring it, then looks back toward area she just left, smiling.)*

Just listen to them sing! They are so happy. And they have a right to be! The Canaanite army and its great general, Sisera, have defeated at last. The Hebrew people now control the important mountain passes at Megiddo and Taanach, not to mention the Valley of Jezreel.

And what am I, Deborah, doing in the midst of this military celebration? Well, it's a rather unusual story —I find it hard to believe myself! *(Rises from bench and paces as she talks.)*

First I must make sure you understand that I didn't seek to be involved in this war. I'm a wife and home-maker from the area of Ramah and Bethel in the hill country, about 50 miles south of here. My husband is Lappidoth. He has herds of animals in the hills. When I was younger I helped him with his work and kept our little house in order. *(Pauses, remembering; smiles, shakes her head.)*

But . . . people started calling me a prophetess after I mentioned my thoughts about the ways of God. I wasn't trying to set myself up as an authority, but God seemed to give me the words to say. Little by little I started having visitors at our home—people who want-ed advice about problems, people who wished to know God's will in their lives, people who wanted a third party to decide their argument. I sat outside our home, receiving visitors under a big palm tree that came to be known as the Palm of Deborah. Lappidoth was very puzzled by all the attention I was receiving, but he understood, as I did, that my ability to visit with the people and give them counsel was a gift from God.

I still kept my home nicely, and on occasion I still helped Lappidoth with the herds. But there was no doubt in my mind that God had a purpose for my life and that he was using me to speak to people. I spent much time in prayer, seeking God's will, because I knew that in and of myself I could not advise or help the people who came to me. The weight of this responsibility was heavy on me. Without my assurance that I was doing God's will, I would have crumbled beneath it. *(Seats herself.)*

This has gone on for many years. Now people from all the tribes come to me for judgment. Lappidoth and I live in the area of the tribe of Ephraim. Near us are the areas of Benjamin, Dan, and Manasseh. Here in the north country the tribes of Issachar, Asher, Zebulun, and Naphtali settled. Way to the south are Judah, Gad, and Reuben. I praise God that he has used me as one of his servants in helping the tribes settle this promised land. *(Restless, rises to walk.)*

But I'm a woman! How many times have I said to God, "I am just a woman, Lord! People will not listen to a woman!" . . . And sometimes I think I hear God laughing softly, because people *have* listened. That's why I'm in the midst of this victory celebration in this military camp.

(Walks to area of singing and listens, then paces

23

back.) They're still singing. They repeat the song over and over. It is recounting the battle and the victory. *(Sits on bench.)*

People ask me how I hear God speak, and I never quite know how to explain it. I don't actually hear a voice, but it's almost as though God has placed the thought or answer in my head, ready-made. I suddenly *know* what he wants me to know. There's an assurance in that knowledge that is very comforting. That carries me through when people doubt and laugh at me.

One day when I was praying, I received an unusual message from God. I knew if I told people about it there would be many doubts and much laughing. God was explaining to me how the Hebrew people would have a great victory over the Canaanite army led by Sisera.

Now that in itself was a wild and perilous idea. Sisera's army consisted of thousands of soldiers, and they had 900 chariots of iron from which to fight. The people of Israel had been under the domination of Jabin, king of Canaan, for 20 years. Now God was telling me that Israel would conquer the Canaanites. Unbelievable! But I proceeded to put God's plan into action.

First I sent a summons to Barak, one of Israel's most capable military men. When Barak came to my home I gave him God's message: "The Lord, the God of Israel, commands you, 'Go, gather your men at Mount Tabor, taking ten thousand from the tribe of Naphtali and the tribe of Zebulun. And I, your Lord, will draw out Sisera, the general of Jabin's army, to meet you by the River Kishon with his chariots and his troops; and I will give him into your hand.'"

At first Barak was skeptical. He knew all about the 900 chariots that Sisera commanded, and he also knew how powerful the Canaanite army was. We talked together about God's command. Was it possible? Barak asked over and over. Was it possible? Time and again I encouraged Barak by reminding him how God had helped the Hebrew people in the past. Remember Joshua and the walls of Jericho, I said. Remember Moses and the waters of the Red Sea. Remember the many battles we fought for this land. Finally Barak's objections were silenced. He said nothing. I was praying inwardly that Barak would find the courage to follow the Lord's command. *(Rises, laughs a little.)*

Well, he found the courage to go into battle all right! But I was really surprised at the form his courage took! "Deborah," Barak said, "if you will go with me, I will go; but if you will not go with me, I will not go."

When I heard Barak's words I could almost hear the Lord saying, "This is *your* challenge, Deborah. What will you do?"

For an instant I thought of Lappidoth and his herds, and I thought of my little home near the Palm of Deborah. I am a wife and homemaker. What am I thinking of—to go to war against the Canaanites? But just as quickly I thought about God's purpose for my life —how he has used me as a judge and counselor in Israel and how he has spoken to the people through me. "Of course I'll go with you, Barak," I said. "Surely I will. Nevertheless, the road on which you are going will not lead to your glory, for the Lord will sell Sisera into the hand of a woman." That was a message God had given me, but I didn't know how or where that would happen. *(Moves around scene as she speaks.)*

Things moved very quickly once Barak decided to follow the Lord's command. We went to Barak's home in Kedesh, and soon he had gathered ten thousand men. From Kedesh Barak moved his troops to Mount Tabor, the place where the Lord had commanded him to go. Mount Tabor is a round hill overlooking the Valley of Jezreel. This valley is beautiful—flat and green. During the past 20 years this valley has been under the control of Jabin and the Canaanites. Their iron chariots roll so easily across the flat land!

I, too, was on Mount Tabor with the troops of Barak, awaiting the signal from the Lord that the battle should begin. I gazed across the Valley of Jezreel, toward Megiddo and Taanach. These were in more hilly and mountainous areas, but the Canaanites controlled them, too. It was easy for the Canaanites to divide the Hebrew people. Some of the tribes were in the southern part of the promised land, while other tribes were in the north. Jabin controlled the Valley of Jezreel and the mountain passes, so we were a weak and helpless people. Our land was divided by the Canaanite occupation. I could see why the Lord had chosen this as the strategic area for battle.

(Becomes quite animated.) The word that Hebrew soldiers were gathered on Mount Tabor quickly

reached Sisera. He called out his 900 chariots of iron and all the men, and they started marching toward Mount Tabor through the Valley of Jezreel.

At just the right moment the Lord put words into my mouth. (*Shouts.*) "Up!" I cried to Barak. "For this is the day in which the Lord has given Sisera into your hand. Does not the Lord go out before you?"

Barak and his ten thousand men went down Mount Tabor to meet Sisera and his soldiers and chariots. I, too, rode with the attack. The Lord was with us!

As we were riding and marching toward Sisera, a storm suddenly came up behind us. Sleet and hail were driving at our backs. But we could see clearly in front of us. As we approached Sisera and his army, we could hear the war cries and the rumble of the iron chariots. "The Lord is with us!" I shouted again and again. I could hear Barak roaring orders to his men. The Hebrew soldiers were giving war cries.

(*Continues to be animated.*) And suddenly I saw what the Lord was doing! The sleet and hail that were at our backs were driving right into the faces of Sisera and his army! Their eyes were blinded by the storm and they were crippled by the biting cold. Barak's army pushed *on* and *on,* seeing that God was aiding them.

(*Remembers gruesomeness of battle.*) Nothing in my experience had prepared me for the slaughter of men and animals in war. It was ugly and gruesome, but on and on Barak pushed, and I could do no less. "The Lord is giving Sisera into our hands!" I cried over and over. "Lord, help us! Lord, help us!" I shouted. And the soliders cried, "Lord, help us!"

Now what was left of Sisera's army was near the Kishon River, and the storm caused the river to rise. Some of the iron chariots were swept away in the rushing flood waters. Other chariots just sank in the mud. Finally all the soldiers and archers and charioteers were dead. We stood there, looking at the devastation. *(Shouts.)* "Praise God!" I cried. The Hebrew soldiers were panting for breath and leaning on their weapons. "Praise the God of Israel who has given the Canaanites into our hands!"

(Looks around, puzzled, suspicious.) But then Barak and I looked at each other. We realized at the same time that we had not seen Sisera, the general, fall to his death. We realized that Sisera must have deserted his troops before the army had been destroyed.

Barak ordered the army to take the Canaanite weapons and return to Mount Tabor. Then Barak and I and a few trusted soldiers started trailing Sisera. Barak thought the Canaanite general might go to Heber the Kenite for help, since there was peace between Jabin and the house of Heber.

We traveled quietly and carefully, watching for an ambush by Sisera. But we journeyed all the way to Heber's campsite, about 20 miles, without seeing anything of Sisera. *(Moves across the scene, as though traveling; creates a new area of action in imaginary campsite.)*

Jael, the wife of Heber the Kenite, met us at the edge of the campsite. "Come," she said, "and I will show you the man you are seeking."

Barak looked at me in surprise. "What would Jael

know of Sisera?" he whispered to me. "Is Sisera so drunk with wine that he didn't notice us coming?" Jael led us to her tent and then motioned Barak to come in. The soldiers and I waited outside. Was Sisera in there? If so, why was he being so quiet?

(With great emotion.) Barak, the great military commander, came out of the tent. His face was deadly white, his eyes staring right past me. He tried to speak but his voice failed him.

"What is it, Barak?" I said, fearful of the answer. I shook his arm. *"Barak,* tell me what's in Jael's tent!"

"Sisera is in there, Deborah," Barak said hoarsely.

"Sisera! How can that be? Unless he's. . . ." *(Pauses as new idea strikes her.)* And suddenly the Lord's message rang clearly through my head. The Lord had said he would deliver Sisera into the hands of a woman.

(In great distress, yet in control of herself.) Barak tried to stop me from going into the tent, but I wanted to see Sisera for myself. Jael was still in the tent, looking at her handiwork. At first I, too, was horrified at the sight. Sisera lay dead, his eyes staring blankly at the tent wall. A large wooden tent peg had been driven completely through his head, into one temple and out the other. Sisera was literally nailed into the ground.

"Jael," I whispered, "did you do that?"

"Yes, I killed him," she said calmly. "I saw him coming into the camp, looking for Heber. All I know is that I had a compulsion to bring him into my tent. I knew that I must kill my enemy. First I gave him milk to drink, and then when he laid down to rest, I saw my opportunity. I waited until he was sleeping. Then I came in here quietly with the tent peg and a hammer, and I pounded the peg into his head. He didn't even move, Deborah. He only opened his eyes, the way you see him now."

It was a horrifying sight. But both Jael and I knew that the Lord had used her to defeat the Canaanite general. We left the tent together, our arms around each other. Barak looked at us. Then he knelt at our feet.

"Daughters of Yahweh," he said respectfully. "Most blessed of women, Jael and Deborah."

(Moves to area of singing again.) And that's what they're singing about! The battle, the Lord's command, how Barak and I led them into victory, how Jael killed Sisera! They're rejoicing in their victory and in the protection of the Lord of Israel.

The status of women in Israel is not high. Many women are little more than slaves or pieces of property. But God used me, and he used Jael, to defeat the Canaanite army which has oppressed us for 20 years! The people are singing our praises.

(Sits down on the bench, weary.) I'm very tired now. More than anything I want to go home. I want to tell Lappidoth what happened and praise God with him. I want to see my house; I want to stand in the shade of the Palm of Deborah. I've traveled far from Ramah and Bethel to carry out the Lord's command. But now . . . it's time to go home. *(Rises slowly and exits in a dignified manner.)*

Hannah

1 Samuel 1—3

Elkanah—el-KAY-nuh
Peninnah—peh-NINE-uh
Shiloh—SHY-low
Eli—EE-lye
Ramah—RAY-muh

Hannah is a middle-aged woman dressed in a bright robe, perhaps one with stripes in it. If possible, she should have a long scarf or a hood on the robe so she can slightly change her appearance at certain points in the drama.

The drama is a prayer in three parts. Hannah defines the three parts by slightly altering her appearance with changes in her dress and also by changing her position in the scene.

The scene also changes, but only by Hannah's words—not by actual physical change. The first part takes place in the house of God in Shiloh; the second part on the road as she returns from a trip to the house of God in Shiloh; and the third part in her home in Ramah. There is no furniture in the scene.

Hannah is a joyous woman who believes

completely in the power of God. The first prayer is one of petition; the second, one of thanksgiving; and the third, one of adoration.

(Hannah walks into the scene and moves to one side of it. She first bows her head, with hands folded, as if in silent prayer. Then she lifts her head and looks slightly upward as she addresses God.)

O Lord of Hosts, I come to you in prayer once again. You know the misery of my life . . . and you know the deepest desire of my heart.

Lord, this is a special day. Elkanah, Peninnah, and I have come to Shiloh to sacrifice to you, as we do every year. I love to come here to your house, O Lord. I feel so close to you when we're here.

I have a confession to make. I've had very ugly feelings about Peninnah again. In truth, Lord, there are times when I hate that woman. She can be so mean to me when she wants to torment me about . . . about the children. *All* the children! O Lord, Peninnah has six sons and daughters now—the newest one just arrived last month. Elkanah is so proud of his new son.

(Covers face with hands for a moment, hiding tears.) O Lord, I don't blame my husband for being proud of his new son. Little Joshua is a beautiful, healthy baby. . . . But Lord, Peninnah already has five other beautiful, healthy children . . . and I have none. I'm older than Peninnah, Lord, and I've been married to Elkanah longer than she has . . . yet Peninnah has many children, and I have none.

(Pauses, deeply grieved.) And, Lord . . . surely you

must hear how she speaks to me about it. Peninnah says terrible things to me. She says Elkanah doesn't really love me, or she laughs and says I'm too old to have children. Sometimes she says that I've sinned in some way, and that you are punishing me, Lord. . . .

(In anguish, her voice is tearful and pleading.) Is that true, O God of Israel? *Are* you punishing me? Have I done some terrible thing? Have I sinned against you in some way hidden to me? *Why* do I not have any children? . . . *(Runs hands over face, miserable.)*

Even here at the sacrifice, the fact of my childlessness shows up again. Peninnah and all her children each get a portion of the sacrifice—and I only get one portion because I'm alone, with no children. Oh, the look that Peninnah gave me this morning when Elkanah handed me my single portion. What triumph gleamed in her eyes!

Sometimes I've been so miserable about it all that I couldn't eat. You know I have to be feeling *terrible* if I don't eat, Lord. . . . Last time it happened Elkanah said to me, "Hannah, why do you weep? And why do you not eat? And why is your heart sad? Am I not more to you than 10 sons?"

(Animated, even angry.) Lord, you know that I love Elkanah with all my heart! And you know that I've tried to please him all these years! And he's a very good man! . . . But, Lord . . . my husband does *not* take the place of a child in my life. You know how desperately and passionately I want a son of my own—a son for Elkanah borne by *me!*

(Determined, calmer.) O Lord of Hosts, I have not

33

come to your house just to whine and complain. I have come with a very special petition, one that I have thought about for a long time. . . . O Lord, if you will look upon my affliction and not forget how much I love you, and if you will give me a son, then I make this vow to you: I will give that son to you all the days of his life, and in honor to you, I will not allow his hair to be cut. . . .

Lord, I know you can work wonders—I know you can change lives. I pray today—here in the house of the Lord in Shiloh—that you will touch me, your humble maidservant, and give me the great gift of a son of my own. Blessed be the name of the Lord of Hosts!

(Bows head in silent prayer. After a moment, slowly moves to other side of stage. Adjusts clothing, taking hood off if it was on, putting it on if it was off, rearranging her long scarf, to convey idea that time has passed and she is now speaking to the Lord at a different time and in a different place. Her face is alive with joy and happiness.)

O Lord, everything went so well today! This is the day I've been dreaming of ever since I knew I would bear a child. Today I brought my young son Samuel to the house of the Lord in Shiloh and dedicated him to your service. I left him with the priest Eli. I know I will feel lonesome without my little son, but when I know that the God of Israel will use Samuel for his glorious purposes—well, I can't be *too* lonesome.

We're resting the animals on our way home to Ramah. I walked over here to the river where I can have some privacy and speak to you in prayer, Lord.

It's hard to pray the way I want to when Elkanah and Peninnah are talking all the time during our journey.

Oh, what a wonderful change in Peninnah, Lord! I've wondered about that often. Did Peninnah change because she saw that I, too, would bear a child, or did she change because of my attitude toward her? I know that many times I would lash out at Peninnah in anger when she did some little thing, and that I spoke to her sharply, acting like I was in total charge of the household. When I'm really honest about it, I have to admit that I made life difficult for Peninnah. She in turn tormented me about my childlessness. . . .

Yes, Lord, you not only gave me the child I so desperately wanted, but you gave me a new attitude and spirit, too. I found so many *good* things about Peninnah and I began to praise her. I was amazed to discover what a good worker she was, and, yes, Lord, what a good *mother* she was!

But, Lord, the greatest day in my life was the day I discovered that I was with child! I had suspected it for a long time, but didn't dare say anything to *anyone*. And then one day I felt little feet and hands begin to kick and punch me from the inside! And I knew a little baby was forming and growing inside my womb!

I prepared a wonderful meal for Elkanah and told him the news. He couldn't believe it—he said that I must be imagining things! But he knows me to be a truthful woman, and finally he had to believe that a child really was on the way! Then we told Peninnah. I already was on much better terms with her, so I really wanted to share the joy with her! And for once

Peninnah was speechless! Then she hugged me as if we were best friends, and, Lord, ever since then we have been exactly that—best friends!

(Pauses, smiles.) And then Samuel was born! Peninnah was right there with me when he came, and immediately she said, "Hannah! It's a big, beautiful boy!" And we cried and laughed and cried some more! Elkanah came in, anxious to see his new son, and I'll never forget how proudly he held Samuel! Suddenly I forgot all the years of pain and sorrow!

But I didn't forget my vow, Lord! This child was yours from the moment he was conceived. I took good care of him during his first four years of life, and now we've brought him to the house of the Lord where he can begin working for you along with the priest Eli. . . . He's so little, but he really does understand a lot, Lord! And I've taught him to love you with all his heart!

Elkanah understands what I'm doing as I give Samuel to you, Lord, and Peninnah has really been so kind about it. Deep down I was afraid she might begin to torment me again, but I needn't have worried. Now we share her children!

And, Lord, perhaps some day . . . perhaps you will again give me the joy of bearing another child. But if not . . . it's all right! I've known your love and mercy, and I've known my son Samuel. That is sufficient joy for your maidservant! Blessed be the name of the Lord of Hosts!

(Hannah joyfully looks upward as she finishes her prayer of praise and thanksgiving. Then she slowly

moves to another spot, probably in the middle of the scene, toward the audience. She again adjusts her clothing, showing a change of time and place. After a pause, she again speaks in prayer. She is happy and joyful, but in a steadier, calmer fashion.)

O Lord, we've just today heard the news! I feel as if I should say that I can't *believe* it—but that's not true. I knew from the very beginning that Samuel was a special person and that you would use him in your service and to your glory, Lord!

Elkanah journeyed to Shiloh on matters of business and he heard people speaking about Samuel in the marketplace. They were saying that the boy Samuel is a prophet of the God of Israel! When Elkanah questioned them, they said they had heard of a special visitation of God upon the boy in the house of the Lord. Elkanah went to speak to Eli about the matter, and learned that you, Lord, indeed have spoken to our son, Samuel, and not only once but many times. Eli said that it certainly seems that you have shown special favor to Samuel and that you will use him as a prophet.

No, Lord, I'm not really surprised about this. The last time we visited Samuel during our yearly sacrifice in Shiloh, he told me about how he sometimes sleeps in the very presence of the ark of the covenant, and how he had been awakened one night by a voice calling him. . . . So it's happened again, and apparently on several occasions.

(Pauses, thinking about her son.) Samuel will soon be twelve years old, Lord. . . . Twelve years ago he came into our lives as a special blessing, and now you

are using him in such a marvelous way. It's been a long time since there's been a prophetic voice in Israel, and now we know that Samuel, our son, is the one chosen to speak for the Lord.

(Turns her head, as if she's heard a sound.) And you've blessed us all in another way, too, Lord! Elkanah and I now have two daughters and three more sons! They know their big brother Samuel is in Shiloh, and they see him once a year when we sacrifice. And we all pray every day for Samuel, knowing that he is favored in your sight, Lord.

And my good friend, Peninnah, Lord—she is such a support to me! I love her as my own sister.

And so, Lord, I come to you today in thanksgiving and adoration! I cannot comprehend the many blessings you've given to me, your maidservant. Thank you for my son Samuel, and for my other wonderful children. Thank you for my loving husband, Elkanah, who cares so well for me and our whole family. Thank you for Peninnah. And, Lord, thank you for all the love and care you have shown to me, even while I was unhappy and complaining. Thank you for using me, your maidservant, for your glorious will.

Blessed be the name of the Lord of hosts!
(Exits.)

Shunammite woman

2 KINGS 4:8-37; 8:1-6

Shunammite—SHOO-nuh-might
Elisha—eh-LYE-shah
Shunem—SHOO-num
Gehazi—geh-HAY-zye
Carmel—CAR-muhl
Philistines—FILL-ih-steens

The Shunammite woman is quite old. She wears
ordinary clothing—a long, plain dress with a rope
tied about her waist.

There is a bench in the scene, but everything
else in the setting is imaginary. It is a bedroom
on the rooftop of the Shunammite woman's house.
There is a narrow cot, a table, and the bench.
There are a couple openings in the walls out of
which the woman occasionally looks.

It is harvest season. The woman and her teenage
son have just returned to their home after a seven-
year absence. She is going to clean this rooftop
room. It is morning.

*(The Shunammite woman enters with a couple of
cleaning cloths. She holds one, using it to wash and*

39

dust, and the other can be handy, looped over her rope belt. She is happy, and eager to clean the room.)

Oh, good! It looks as if this room has fared very well in our absence! I was afraid it would be damaged by wind or rain, or even animals, but it seems all right!

(Moves about, washing furniture.) Seven years! I can hardly believe we've been gone that long! When I'm back in this house and in this room, it just seems like yesterday since . . . since. . . . *(Pauses and freezes in position, as if remembering.)*

Oh, this room is so full of memories! *(Smiles.)* This was the room that Elisha used, and this was the room where he promised me a son. This was the room where Joel was. . . . *(Seems at loss for words; sits down on bench.)*

This . . . room. . . . My husband built this room on the rooftop of our home when I asked him to make a special place for the prophet Elisha. The prophet would pass through our little village of Shunem every now and again, and I would invite him into our home to eat. After a while he got into the habit of coming here, and he would stop without urging from one of my servants.

We so much enjoyed having Elisha here. He would teach us about the God of Israel, and he would tell us about God's powerful works. I was strengthened and inspired every time Elisha was here, and the prophet seemed to appreciate the food and companionship.

(Gets up and goes to walls, feeling them lightly, then looks around the room as she speaks.) One day I said to my husband, "Behold now, I can perceive that

this is a holy man of God, who is continually passing our way. Let us make a small roof chamber with walls, and put there for him a bed, a table, a chair, and a lamp, so that whenever he comes to us, he can go in there." And this room is the result!

(Goes to openings in wall and looks through them.) I remember how surprised Elisha was when the room was ready. I saw him coming down the road with his servant Gehazi, and I ran to meet him. I told him all about the special resting place we had made for him. Then I brought him up here and showed him every-thing *(gestures)*—the bed, the table, the lamp, the chair, everything! Elisha really liked this place because it was quiet and cool. He often came here.

(Goes toward entryway.) One day . . . one day some-thing very extraordinary happened! Elisha and Gehazi had been alone in the room for a while, and then Ge-hazi called me to come. I stood in the doorway. *(Pretends to stand in doorway, looking into room.)* And I heard Elisha say the most incredible words: "At this season next year, when the time comes round, you shall embrace a son." My first reaction was one of pain and disbelief. I said, "No, my lord, O man of God; do not lie to your maidservant." You see, *(goes to sit on bench)* I had never been able to have children. My husband and I had been married for many years and I always felt the stigma of childlessness. My husband was very kind about it, but I knew it made him sad. Every man wants sons to carry on his name. And I was barren. It was like a curse on me.

So when Elisha promised that I would have a child,

41

I couldn't bear the idea of hoping for such a thing and then being disappointed. There were too many times already when I had thought I was carrying a child, and then I had been cruelly disappointed. I just couldn't bring myself to believe his words. The prophet explained that he and Gehazi appreciated this quiet, cool room so much that they tried to think of some way to ask God to reward me, and they decided that what I wanted most was a son.

(Stands, paces.) Well, they were right about that, of course. I sometimes allowed myself to dream of having a son. . . . *(Smiles, delighted.)*

But a year later I didn't have to dream anymore—our beautiful son Joel was born! It was a miracle! My husband was like a young colt—running here and there telling everyone the good news! . . . What a beautiful baby he was! Elisha often visited. He loved to pick up the boy and play with him. When Joel was older Elisha would tell him stories about the God of Israel. . . . And so our life continued for about 10 years. Joel grew to be a strong, happy boy.

(Goes back to bench, sits down; becomes dejected.) I still can't believe what happened that day. In the morning I had sent Joel out to work with his father, reaping the harvest. There were a lot of reapers and Joel liked to be with them all. But this day, something happened to the boy. My husband told me that Joel came to him the middle of the morning complaining about pain in his head: "Oh, my head, my head!" Joel cried.

Well, his father immediately had one of the servants

carry Joel back here to the house. I sat with the boy on my lap, rocking him, rocking him, trying to make him feel better. But I could tell he was burning up with fever. I gave him water—but nothing helped. At noontime . . . Joel died in my arms.

(Buries face in hands, shakes head back and forth.) I could not believe he was dead at first. I thought he'd just gone to sleep. But soon I could see I was just fooling myself—the boy was dead.

(Stands and goes to doorway.) Something in me believed Joel was dead and something else said, "Maybe he's not dead for all time." I still don't know how I did all the things I did, but I believe God was in control, helping and guiding me. . . . First I brought Joel up here to Elisha's room. *(Gestures toward bed.)* I laid him carefully on the bed. It was the safest place I could think of. Then I closed the door.

(Moves around room, gesturing for emphasis.) Then I called to my husband: "Send me one of the servants and one of the donkeys, that I may quickly go to the man of God, and come back again." My husband was puzzled by this request since it wasn't a Sabbath day or a day of new moon or a holiday, but he sent the servant and the donkey anyway. Quickly I saddled the animal and told the servant, "Urge the beast on; do not slacken the pace for me unless I tell you."

I knew Elisha would be praying and worshiping at Mount Carmel. That's about 20 miles from Shunem, and it was the longest ride I've ever made. All I could think was, "If I can find Elisha and have him touch Joel, everything will be all right." It wasn't that I thought Elisha had power in himself to do such a miraculous thing, but I knew he was in constant touch with God. If anyone on this earth could help Joel, it was Elisha.

We traveled on and on. The servant hurried the donkey along, and I prayed to the God of Israel that we would not be too late. Oh, 20 miles . . . 20 long miles. . . . It seemed as if I were traveling all the way to the holy city of Jerusalem itself!

Finally I saw the place on Mount Carmel where Elisha stays. I kept my eye on that spot, urging the beast and the servant on. "Hurry, hurry!" I cried. "We're almost there!"

When Elisha saw me coming he sent Gehazi to meet me. "Is it well with you? Is it well with your husband? Is it well with the child?" the servant asked me. But I didn't want to disturb Gehazi. "It is well," I said. My sights were on Elisha in the distance.

When I finally reached Elisha I fell at his feet in utter exhaustion. I grabbed hold of his feet, partly because I wished to implore him to help us and partly because I didn't want him to get away from me. Gehazi became quite alarmed when he saw this and tried to protect Elisha. But the prophet sensed something was terribly wrong. "Let her alone, for she is in bitter distress; and the Lord has hidden it from me, and has not told me," he told Gehazi. Then he gently said to me, "What is wrong, woman of Shunem?"

I couldn't bring myself to say Joel was dead. Instead I said, "Did I ask my lord for a son? Did I not say, Do not deceive me?" It hurt so much to think that this special boy had been given to me, and now had been taken away. The prophet seemed to know exactly what was wrong, even though I didn't say it in so many words. Elisha gave his staff to Gehazi and told him to hurry to my house and lay the staff on the boy's face in an effort to awaken him. But I just knew that Elisha had to come to Shunem, and I would not leave Mount Carmel without him—not if he sent 100 Gehazis to my house!

I was right, too. Elisha finally came with me, and even while we were traveling the 20 miles back to Shunem, Gehazi came to us and told Elisha that nothing had changed—Joel was still dead.

When we finally reached my house Elisha came into this upper room alone. I remained below, praying and hoping that this man of God could bring about the miracle I longed for—the return of my beautiful son Joel. Gehazi and I waited and waited. We could hear movement in the room above, then it would be silent. Then there was movement again. And then . . . then I heard something that was so beautiful! I heard Joel sneezing! I recognized his sneezes because I had worried about them so many times before, but *this* time the sneezes were *beautiful!* Elisha called Gehazi and me to the room, and sure enough—Joel was sitting up on the bed *(gestures to bed)*, rubbing his nose and his eyes.

"Take up your son," Elisha said. First I fell to the prophet's feet in thanksgiving, and then I ran to the bed, taking Joel in my arms. How warm and wonderful he felt. His arms clung to my neck and he whispered in my ear, "Mother, I'm so hungry!"

I took Joel right downstairs and gave him some bread and goat's milk. I couldn't take my eyes off him. His eyes were dancing, and his hair was tousled—just the way it's been since he was born. And now he was alive! God had given my son back to me!

(*Walks to bed.*) Later Elisha told me that he had prayed to God for the boy's life, and then the prophet had laid his whole body on top of Joel's body, putting his mouth on Joel's mouth, and his eyes on his eyes, and his hands on his hands. Elisha said he could feel the boy's cold flesh starting to get warm. Then Elisha got up and walked around the room, praying again for the boy. Once more Elisha stretched himself out on the child, and it was then that Joel sneezed seven times and opened his eyes. Elisha told me that the sight of that child opening his eyes and the feeling of motion beneath his old body was one of the most inspiring moments of his life. Elisha has always loved Joel—he's been a special child to him—and he felt blessed joy to see him come back to life.

(*Starts to clean room again with cloths.*) Quite a few years have passed since Joel was raised from death. So much has happened. Elisha warned us about a famine that would come in the land and told us to leave for a safer place. Joel, my husband, and I traveled to the coastlands where the Philistines live, and we spent the last seven years there. It wasn't the best life, but at least we were able to eat.

My old husband had become very weak and ill. He died while we were there, so Joel and I were left alone. . . . But now we're back and the king has restored our house and land to us, even though they'd been taken over by the king's soldiers. They even gave me the produce of the fields, and it's enough to feed Joel and me until another harvest.

Joel is a man now—he's 18 years old! So he takes care of me. . . . *(Starts walking to doorway of scene.)* But I haven't forgotten how I carried him up to this room, and how Elisha raised him from death by God's power. I haven't forgotten that sweet little child who sneezed and rubbed his eyes as he came back to life. I haven't forgotten to thank the God of Israel every single day for the miracle of life he's given to me—not just once, but twice. What a miracle!

Queen Esther

THE BOOK OF ESTHER

Haman—HAY-mun
Persia—PUR-zhuh
Mordecai—MORE-deh-kye
Ahasuerus—ah-ha-SAIR-uhs
Susa—SOO-zah

Queen Esther is a young woman dressed elegantly in a long robe. She is wearing jewelry, perhaps with a tiara in her hair.

(Esther enters and begins preparing for a meal for her husband, the king, and for Haman. She is anxious about the meal and confrontation to come.)

Now I wonder if I have remembered everything. I have the golden plates and the golden goblets. A tender young lamb is roasting, and the king's favorite delicacies have been prepared.

(Moves around imaginary table.) The table looks beautiful! The white flowers against the blue linen make such a lovely contrast. The king's favorite couch is here, so he has a good view into the garden court.

So much depends on this banquet. I am terrified to think what will happen if the king denies my request. If Haman has his way, every Jew in Persia will be destroyed. But I mustn't think about that. I must concentrate on pleasing the king so he will listen to my appeal.

(Becomes thoughtful.) Mordecai says that perhaps God has placed me in the position of queen just for this purpose—to intercede for my people. And perhaps my dear cousin is right. Unless God had planned it, how else could I have found such favor with King Ahasuerus?

I remember the day I was brought to the palace. I was so frightened. And so were the hundreds of other girls from all over the kingdom. We just didn't know what to expect. All we knew was that the king would pick one of us to be his queen.

I hadn't realized that the preparations would take so long. There was a 12-month beautification period. For six months oil of myrrh was used on our skin and during the other six months special ointments and spices were used. At the end of the year each girl was brought before the king and he was expected to make his choice.

I was so surprised when King Ahasuerus chose me! He set the royal crown on my head and then gave a great banquet in my honor for all the princes and servants. The king even granted a remission in taxes to the provinces and he gave many royal gifts.

I wonder if the king would have chosen me if he had known that I am Jewish. I couldn't understand why

Mordecai didn't want me to tell the king right away. Why should I keep such a thing from him? But no—Mordecai made me promise to keep the identity of my people a secret. Even now the king doesn't know of the relationship between Mordecai and me. All he knows of Mordecai is that he is an official at the palace gate. And it's written in the record of memorable deeds, of course, how Mordecai saved the king's life.

And now *this!* Will Mordecai and all the rest of us be killed simply because we are Jews? Haman—what an evil man he is! The king gave him a very high position in the government, a seat above all the princes. Everyone was to honor Haman and pay their respects. But Mordecai remembered that God had said we were to worship no one save God alone. He refused to bow down to Haman. Haman became so furious that he plotted to destroy every Jew in Persia.

I've heard that Haman took a whole year to decide on a favorable day to kill the Jews. They say that lots were cast in front of Haman month after month until he could ascertain just the right day.

Haman is so clever. He tricked the king into believing that the Jews were a threat to the kingdom and that they must all be killed. The thirteenth day of the twelfth month has been set for the destruction. My people are fasting and weeping, wearing sackcloth and ashes. I, too, have been fasting. But there's one thing—one thing that may save us. Haman doesn't know that I, the queen, am a Jew.

As soon as the word spread that the Jews were to be killed, Mordecai sent me word to go to the king immediately and beg him to change the command. But Mordecai must have forgotten that no one is to approach the king in the inner court without being called. Anyone who comes to him without permission is to be put to death, unless the king holds out the golden scepter to him. And the king hadn't called for me in 30 days.

When Mordecai heard this, he had a very sharp answer for me. "Don't believe for a minute that just because you live in the palace you will escape death," he said. "If you keep silent now, the Jews will be saved in another way and you and your family will perish. How do you know that you haven't come to the kingdom for such a time as this?"

Right away I asked Mordecai to gather all the Jews from Susa together and hold a fast in my behalf. After three days I would go to the king, whether he had called me or not. If he would have me killed for coming to him, so be it.

(Smiles as she remembers.) But the king is gracious and kind. Yesterday when he saw me standing in the court, he held out the golden scepter to me and said, "What is it, Queen Esther? What is your request? Even if you want half my kingdom, I will give it to you."

Oh, I was tempted to tell him right then what I so desperately wanted, but something told me to be very cautious. I was dealing with powerful and sinister forces. Instead, I invited the king and Haman to come to a dinner I had prepared for them. The king was delighted, and I could see that Haman too was very pleased at the invitation. He had no idea of what I was planning. I wanted him to be perfectly confident of my trust in him.

At the dinner the king again asked me for my wish, but I put him off once more, saying only that I wanted both him and Haman to come the next day to another banquet. That banquet will be held here in just a few minutes.

But last night, Haman took steps to silence Mordecai forever. He erected a gallows from which he swore Mordecai would hang. How he hates Mordecai!

But a strange thing happened during the night. The king couldn't sleep. He had the book of memorable deeds brought to him. There he found it written how Mordecai had saved his life. Two men in the palace had been planning to kill the king, and Mordecai had overheard them plotting together. The king remembered then that Mordecai had never been fittingly honored for his deed, and when morning came he made Haman bestow honors upon Mordecai. Now Haman must hate Mordecai more than ever!

(Turns sharply toward her left, as if she's heard something.) Oh, my guests are coming! *(Gives quick prayer.)* O God of Israel, give your servant strength!

(Smiling, gracious, bows to imaginary guests.) My king, how happy I am that you have come to my banquet once again! And Haman, I'm delighted you could be with us! Your wife and children—are they well? . . . Won't you come to the table? The dinner is ready. Roast lamb, juicy pomegranates, dates, wine. . . . Please, eat your fill. I have so much food prepared. . . . *(Serves guests.)*

Haman, more wine? . . . I'm so glad you're enjoying it, my king! . . . My request, O king, my request?

(Pleading, desperate; moves in beseeching manner, gesturing frequently.) If I have found favor in your sight, O king, and if it pleases you, let life be given to me and to my people. I, Esther, your queen . . . I am a Jew. We are *sold,* my people and I, to be destroyed, to be slain, to be *annihilated!* . . .

Oh, yes, my king, it *is* true! A foe and an enemy has tricked you. *(Points accusingly at imaginary Haman.)* This wicked Haman! *He* is the one! . . . Yes, *you,* Haman! *You* are the enemy!

(Turns to king, beseechingly.) Oh, my king, have mercy on us! *(Takes listening, suspended attitude, then shows great relief.)*

Oh, thank you, my king! You are merciful and good!

(Turns partly away, with hands prayerfully clasped.) And I thank my God. . . .

(Turns head, as if watching people leave room.) The guards are taking Haman to be hung on the gallows he built for Mordecai. What a bitter harvest he has reaped! What was it the king said? That Mordecai would be given Haman's position? . . . Yes, and he also promised that the Jews would be safe in Persia.

My people, my people . . . what heartache we have known. Not only here and now, but in so many times and so many places. But the God of Israel is mighty. As in times past, he has delivered us again!

(Comes to attention, after musing.) But why am I standing here? I must find Mordecai and tell him the glorious news! *(Exits in a joyful hurry.)*

Ruth

THE BOOK OF RUTH

Obed—OH-bed
Naomi—nay-OH-mih
Mahlon—MAWL-un
Chilion—CHILL-eon
Moab—MOE-ab
Orpah—OAR-puh
Moabite—MOE-ah-bite
Boaz—BOE-az

Ruth is young and vibrant. She is dressed in a long white gown, perhaps with another robe thrown around her or with a shawl wrapped around her. The costume is meant to suggest nightclothes.

Two benches are set in the middle of the scene at angles to one another, suggesting a seating arrangement. A low box or simple cradle may be used to represent the baby's bed, or the bed may be imaginary.

The time is about midnight.

(Ruth has been awakened by her baby's cries. She is anxious. She comes hurrying into the scene.) Ohhh,

my poor baby! What is the matter? *(Reaches into cradle to pick up imaginary baby, rocks him in her arms.)* There, there. . . . Don't cry, little Obed. . . .

(Suddenly becomes aware of a problem.) Oh! Oh, no! You're so hot! You're burning up with fever! *(Places baby back in bed and goes to other side of scene to gather imaginary water and cloths. Comes back to his bed.)*

You're burning up, my poor baby! . . . Here, mother is going to put these cool cloths on you. *(Puts imaginary cloths on baby.)* These will help you, little Obed. . . . Oh, don't cry! You're going to feel better now.

(Picks up crying baby, adjusts cloths, then rocks baby, crooning to him.) Poor baby, poor little Obed.

(Suddenly Ruth's attention is drawn to one side of scene. Through Ruth's eyes we see Naomi come into room.) Naomi! . . . Oh, I'm so sorry we awakened you! . . . Yes, it's well past midnight, I'm afraid. Obed has a fever, Naomi. His skin is so hot and dry. I'm afraid it's a very high fever.

(Ruth holds out baby for Naomi's inspection, then gives baby to Naomi.) All right, you take him if you wish. I'll get more cool water and we'll change these cloths. *(Moves to side of scene to gather water and supplies. Returns to Naomi and Obed.)*

There . . . now you hold him and I'll apply these cold cloths to his head . . . and on his arms. . . . And here, I'll put one across his chest. *(Acts out her words, then sits down on one of the benches and talks to Naomi as if she's seating herself on the other.)*

Yes, sit down with him, Naomi. I'll change the cloths

in a moment. . . . What do you think can be the matter with him? He was fine when I put him to bed a few hours ago. Now he's so hot and so miserable. Poor baby, can't even tell us what's wrong—all he can do is cry.

(Gets up, anxious. Walks around benches.) Oh, Naomi, I get so worried when Obed is sick. I can't help remembering . . . well, *you* know. . . . Obed is so precious to me. After losing my husband Mahlon I never thought I'd marry again, and I certainly never dreamed I'd have children. . . . And you, Naomi, you've said so often that Obed is like a gift from God, a replacement for your two sons, Mahlon and Chilion. . . .

(Goes to get more water and returns to bench.) Here, little Obed, mother wants to put colder cloths on you. *(Adjusts cloths on baby in Naomi's arms.)*

Well, he seems a little quieter anyway, Naomi. He likes it when you rock him like that. Maybe if he sleeps a little it will help the fever. . . .

(Sits on bench again.) Yes, he really has quieted down. Maybe you could put him back in his bed. . . . You're right, he'd probably wake up when you put him down. Well, I guess we'll have to sit here and wait!

Naomi, do you ever think about Moab and our life there? . . . Yes, I do, too. I remember my childhood there, but mostly I remember the life we all had together—you, me and Mahlon, Orpah and Chilion. Those were such happy days. . . . Remember how we worked in the fields, and how we'd laugh and play tricks on one another? Oh, it was wonderful! I felt so comfortable with you all, even though you and your sons were from Judah, and Orpah and I were from Moab. For once those national lines didn't seem to matter!

(Happy as she remembers; then her face saddens.) But the happy times didn't last, did they, Naomi?

(Suddenly stands and walks around.) It was like this, do you remember? Of course you do—how could either of us forget? . . . First it was Chilion who had that high fever. Orpah nursed him day and night—oh, we all helped! But in three days he was dead. . . . And then, then Mahlon became ill. Naomi, I really thought that Mahlon had a chance after he lived past three days. But after five days of suffering, he died too. . . . And you, Naomi, you had lost your husband 10 years earlier. It was hard to believe—all the men gone.

(Leans over the baby.) Is he still sleeping? Is he still hot? . . . Yes, he's still very warm, isn't he, but at least he's sleeping. . . .

(Sits on bench opposite Naomi.) And our trip to Bethlehem—remember how we struggled across the Judean wilderness to get back here, Naomi? Oh, that was so bad. And I was so glad I was with you. . . . You're right—you would not have survived the trip alone. And to think you tried to make me stay in Moab!

Oh, yes, I certainly remember our first days here in Bethlehem! Life was so hard—I picked up the grain in the fields after the harvest, and we managed to exist on that. And I felt for quite a while that the people didn't really accept me as a Moabite, that they didn't want

57

me here. But you took care of all that, Naomi! You helped me contact Boaz because of the tradition of a widow marrying the next of kin. Now Boaz and I have this beautiful baby boy!

(Leans over baby.) What do you think, Naomi? Should I get more cold cloths? . . . Yes, you're right. Let him sleep.

(Stands up and stretches, yawning.) Oh, I could go to sleep right here! Did you spend nights like this with Mahlon and Chilion, Naomi? . . . Being a first-time mother, I'm not used to all the worry and the sleepless nights. . . .

(Jerks around and stares at the bench where Naomi and Obed are.) Oh, he's awake again. Why does he cry so hard? *(Goes to bench and reaches for baby.)* Here, I'll take him, Naomi. Your arms must be breaking after holding him so long.

(Takes baby and starts to pace, crooning soft words to crying child.) Poor sweet baby, you're so hot. . . . Oh, good you've got more cold cloths. I'm going to lay him in his bed and take off all his clothes. *(Acts out her words.)* There, now let's put on those fresh, cold cloths. . . . Naomi, I'm really frightened! Why won't this fever break? It seems to be even higher than it was before he went to sleep!

(Steps back from bed and watches baby. Starts weeping.) Naomi, is he going to die? Will he die like Mahlon and Chilion?

(Listens, then nods. Steps to side of scene.) You're right, I was so worried I forgot to pray. . . . Lord of Israel, I beg you for my son's life. We love Obed so

much. He's so precious to us. In your mercy, Lord of Israel, hear us. . . .

Naomi . . . maybe God won't listen to me, because I'm not of the house of Israel. . . . Of course I've accepted him as my God, but maybe. . . .

(Hurries to bed and kneels by it.) He's still crying, Naomi. He's still so hot. . . . Oh, Naomi, you pray for Obed. I don't think I can even say the right words. I'm so frightened!

(Kneels by bed silently for a few moments.) What did you say about Obed? . . . What do you mean, Naomi?

(Stands, as if to talk face to face with Naomi.) I know he's a special baby, Naomi, you don't have to tell me that. . . . You believe God has special plans for this baby? What kind of plans? . . . You think that he's a special baby and God will protect him? . . . Oh, if only I could believe that, Naomi!

(Goes back to bed and reaches in to touch Obed.) Naomi . . . Naomi! I think he's cooler! I really think his skin is cooler! Come and touch him! . . . Don't you think so? So do I!

(Picks up baby.) Come, little one, you're going to feel better now. . . . See, Naomi! His eyes are brighter, and he's not crying. Obed's going to be all right!

(Places baby back in bed, tucking him in.) I really think he'll sleep now. . . . See? He's not fussing any more. Oh, Naomi, do you really think it's true, that God has special plans for Obed? I know he's a beautiful gift to you and me and Boaz. Maybe God will use Obed for a special gift to other people, too.

Good night, Naomi. Get some sleep. Thank you for helping us. I'm just going to check on Obed once more.

(Goes back to the bed and gazes at Obed, then looks directly at audience and says:) Ruth lived in the days of the judges of Israel. She did not know about the Messiah. The promises from the prophets came much later. But Ruth and Obed played a role in God's plans nevertheless. Ruth's son, Obed, became the father of Jesse, and Jesse was the father of King David. Jesus Christ was of the house and lineage of David. Obed was indeed a special baby, one for whom God had special plans in salvation history.

(Looks again at baby, then leaves scene.)

Mary, mother of Jesus (I)

(After the Annunciation, before the Birth)

LUKE 1:5-56; ISAIAH 9:6-7

Zechariah—zek-ah-RYE-ah
Abijah—uh-BYE-juh

Mary is a young girl, perhaps about 15 years of age. She is dressed in a light-colored robe caught about her waist with a light-colored sash. She is wearing a head covering which she can place over her shoulders when it's not being used as a head protector. This can be a large, triangular piece of cloth and should be of a darker color. She is carrying a little bundle, perhaps a knapsack.

Mary is traveling back to Nazareth from the city in the hill country of Judah where Elizabeth and Zechariah live. She has just spent three months with her cousin, Elizabeth.

The scene is outdoors. Something for Mary to sit down and rest on is necessary. This could be a wooden bench, which is described in the drama as an old log.

(Mary enters, happy and eager to return to Nazareth but tired and delighted to spy a log to rest on.)

61

Oh, look at that—just what I need! A place to rest! *(Goes immediately to bench and sits down, sighing in relief as she relaxes.)*

Oh, that's wonderful. I've been walking all morning through the hill country, and this old log is just like a gift. I'll rest here awhile and eat the lunch Elizabeth sent with me. *(Opens knapsack and pretends to eat. Speaks as she eats.)*

This bread tastes very good. I think I've finally learned how to make it properly. Three months of learning the finer arts of cooking from my cousin Elizabeth ought to please Joseph when we're finally married!

(Continues to eat. Pauses to think.) I wonder when we will be married. . . . I wonder if Joseph will want to marry me now. *(Puts down food and knapsack and gets up. Wanders to side of scene. Looks out on imaginary countryside.)*

Nazareth is just over that hill. I'm not very far from home at all, and yet . . . in some ways I feel as if I could be on the other side of the great sea. It may be asking too much of Joseph to understand that . . . that I'm. . . . *(Slowly returns to bench and sits.)*

And my parents . . . my mother. . . . Oh, how I wish Elizabeth could have come home with me to help me explain. But Elizabeth is just about to have a baby herself. She won't be able to travel for quite a while, especially since she's so much older and just having her first baby.

(Smiles as she remembers.) It's been so much fun to be with Elizabeth while she's expecting. She had long

ago given up hope of ever having a baby of her own, but soon she'll be a mother! Elizabeth says the baby is very active. He seems to want to get going in this world!

Zechariah is very proud, of course. He can't speak at all, but his eyes shine as he points to Elizabeth's *very* large midsection and then points to the sky, as if to say that God has given them the baby. Elizabeth says that's exactly what has happened. As a priest of the division of Abijah, Zechariah was serving his turn in the temple when an angel of the Lord appeared to him. Imagine! An angel of the Lord! *(Smiles and shakes her head in wonderment.)* The angel told Zechariah that Elizabeth would have a baby and that it would be a boy who would serve the Lord in a very special way.

Zechariah had trouble believing the news, since both he and Elizabeth are quite old, so the angel gave Zechariah a sign: He will not be able to speak until the child is born! And it's true—Zechariah is not able to speak a word. He communicates by writing on clay tablets or pieces of broken pottery, and by sign language. Elizabeth says that she knows this baby must be very special, since all this has happened!

(Rises and walks to look over hills.) I was amazed when I arrived at Elizabeth's house. . . . I was amazed that Elizabeth knew . . . knew about me.

(Pauses, finds it difficult to speak of these things.) You see . . . I myself had not known of God's purpose in my life for more than a few days. . . . An angel of the Lord had appeared to me also. That sounds so . . .

presumptuous to say that an angel appeared. But it's true. The angel had a very special message for me.

(Slowly walks back to middle of scene. Faces audience.) The Jewish people have long awaited the promised Messiah. Everyone has ideas about how he'll come and who he'll be. Jewish women hope and pray that one of their sons will be the special one. Jewish mothers of girls hope and pray that their daughters will bear the Messiah.

My mother has spoken of this, but always in a matter-of-fact way. It's something that mothers say because it's been said for so long. They all know that the Messiah will be born in a palace, because he'll be a strong and powerful king.

But the angel told me that I, Mary of Nazareth, will be the mother of the Son of the Most High. . . . I can remember every word that angel said to me.

First he said, "Hail, O favored one, the Lord is with you!" I was really frightened, and I wondered about his greeting. But the angel said, "Do not be afraid, Mary, for you have found favor with God. And behold, you will conceive in your womb and bear a son, and you shall call his name Jesus."

(Walks about scene as she explains.) And then the angel said, "He will be great, and will be called the Son of the Most High; and the Lord will give to him the throne of his father David, and he will reign over the house of Jacob for ever; and of his kingdom there will be no end."

I knew from the description that this baby was to be the Messiah. I had been taught the prophecies from the time I was little. Most girls don't know a great deal about these things, but my father knew I was interested and always taught me what he taught my brothers. I know there's a passage in Isaiah's prophecy which says, "For to us a child is born, to us a son is given; and the government will be upon his shoulder, and his name will be called 'Wonderful Counselor, Mighty God, Everlasting Father, Prince of Peace.' Of the increase of his government and of peace there will be no end, upon the throne of David, and over his kingdom, to establish it, and to uphold it with justice and with righteousness from this time forth and for evermore."

But even though I know the prophecies and believe them, I found myself questioning the angel: "How can this be, since I have no husband?"

And the angel answered: "The Holy Spirit will come upon you, and the power of the Most High will overshadow you; therefore the child to be born will be called holy, the Son of God."

(Sits down on bench.) I cannot tell you when that happened. . . . All I know is that I am with child, and in human terms there is no reason why I should be. Although I am betrothed to Joseph we are not yet married, and I do not live in his house. But the fact remains that I am expecting a baby. I know the physical symptoms women experience when they are pregnant, and I find those signs in myself. My cousin Elizabeth confirms these signs, too.

The angel had more to tell me: "And behold, your kinswoman Elizabeth in her old age has also conceived a son; and this is the sixth month with her who was called barren. For with God nothing will be impossible."

(Stands, looks up, holding out her hands, palms up.)
I said, "Behold, I am the handmaid of the Lord; let it be to me according to your word." And then the angel left.

(Moves about.) I did not tell anyone about the visit of the angel or of his message. It just didn't seem right to share that precious news with anyone, not even my mother or Joseph. The thing I had firmly fixed in my mind was that I must go to see Elizabeth. And so I left for her home in the hill country in just a few days.

As I said before, I was amazed that Elizabeth already knew about me. And she told me in such a dramatic fashion! As soon as I entered the home of Zechariah and Elizabeth, I greeted them with words from my family. And Elizabeth cried out, "Blessed are you among women, and blessed is the fruit of your womb! And why is this granted me, that the mother of my Lord should come to me? For behold, when the voice of your greeting came to my ears, the babe in my womb leaped for joy. And blessed is she who believed that there would be a fulfillment of what was spoken to her from the Lord." Elizabeth was filled with God's Spirit as she said those words, and we all wept and praised the God of Israel for his power and love.

I spent three months with Elizabeth, helping her all I could. And she taught me many things that will be important when I marry Joseph. . . . *(Her face clouds over, shows concern.)*

I wonder what will happen when I tell my parents

and Joseph about the baby. I'll tell them the truth, but the truth sounds so strange. Perhaps Joseph will divorce me. . . .

(Worried and frightened.) Perhaps my parents will disown me! . . . If they think I've committed adultery, I could be killed! . . . *(Takes a deep breath and calms herself.)*

Now that's silly. God will protect me. It won't be easy to explain all this, but God's plan is sure, and he will take care of me.

(Picks up bag and prepares to leave.) Well, I've eaten my lunch and I'm rested. It's time to return to Nazareth and all that awaits me there.

(Lifts her face to sky.) My soul magnifies the Lord, and my spirit rejoices in God my Savior, for he has regarded the low estate of his handmaiden. For behold, henceforth all generations will call me blessed; for he who is mighty has done great things for me, and holy is his name. *(Exits.)*

The innkeeper's wife

LUKE 2:1-20; MICAH 5:2; ISAIAH 11:1-2

Caleb—KAY-leb
Nathan—NAY-thin
Leah—LEE-ah

The innkeeper's wife wears a long dress of dark,
ordinary fabric, with an apron-like garment
wrapped around. She carries a cloth and broom.
She gives an occasional swipe with the cloth at
imaginary dust and a push of the broom at
imaginary dirt.

She is peppy, volatile, and frequently paces,
gesturing as she speaks.

*(The innkeeper's wife enters hurriedly, out of
breath.)* Oh, my! I've got to rest a minute! I'll stay
back here where Caleb can't see me. *(Peeks around
imaginary corner to check on Caleb's whereabouts.)*
The people on the rooftop will just have to wait awhile
longer for their meal. . . . Ohhhh, whatever has happened to the Bethlehem I used to know? It was so
peaceful before the Romans marched in.

(Suddenly realizes she's addressing an audience.)

Oh, pardon me! I'm Leah. My husband—he's the fat one with the bald head over there *(gestures around corner)*—he owns this inn. We aren't usually this busy, but the last few weeks have been *terrible!* It's this census that the Roman emperor has ordered. Can you imagine? Everyone has to go to the town where his ancestors came from, so all the people can be counted and registered. Sounds like a lot of nonsense to me, but what do I know?

Caleb is so happy for the business that he's falling all over himself to cram as many people into the inn as possible. That means that Leah runs and runs, and climbs and climbs, and cooks and cooks, and cleans and cleans! *(Becomes breathless thinking about all her work, then becomes confiding.)*

Do you know—Caleb had so many guests packed in last night that he sent some people down to the *stable* to sleep! I couldn't *believe* it when he told me to send Nathan down to clear it out! "Caleb," I said, "are you out of your mind? That stable is in no condition to have people in it!"

But I knew it was useless to argue, so I took some food and water down there. It's behind the inn, built into the hill. I grumbled to myself all the way down there. It wasn't enough that I had to run up and down to the rooftop. Now I had to run up and down the hill, too!

(Her voice softens and her face becomes loving.) But when I saw those people in the stable, my heart went out to the girl. Mary, her name was, from Nazareth. Imagine! From Nazareth! That's all of 70 miles

north! And her in that condition! . . . Listen, I've had eight children myself, and I wouldn't wish a 70-mile donkey ride on my worst enemy if she was about to have a baby!

My, she was so pale and tired, but she didn't complain at all. Me! I'd be raising the roof! . . . And Joseph, her husband, was so kind to her. I helped him make a bed for her on the hay and sent Nathan up the hill for a warm blanket. There wasn't much else we could do. I hated to leave her. I knew it wouldn't be long before that baby came, but I had all the other guests to feed and take care of.

(Pauses a moment and ponders.) It was almost midnight before I had a chance to get back to the stable. Caleb was sleeping by that time, and everything was pretty quiet. But it was so *bright* outside! There was one gorgeous star hanging over the town. It seemed like I could just reach up and touch it.

And do you know what? Mary's baby had been born sometime during the evening! There he was, lying in a manger full of hay. He was wrapped in swaddling cloths that Mary had brought along. Joseph had found that little manger way back in the stable and cleaned it up for the baby. It made a perfect little bed. And Mary looked so beautiful and happy! She sat close to the manger, watching every move that baby made.

(Almost at a loss for words to explain her feelings.) I . . . I can't explain it. . . . There was such an air of peace and joy in that old stable. . . . Some of the animals were standing in the back, watching all the activity . . . and grass roots were growing through the

ceiling. . . . But it didn't seem to make any difference at all. We could have been in one of Solomon's golden palaces!

(Pauses, again remembering.) And then the strangest thing happened. Some shepherds from the hills outside of town came to the stable door. Joseph talked to them quietly and then let them in. The men of the hills crept over to look at the new baby. They fell to their knees, and one of them said to Mary, "The angel of the Lord told us that we would find the baby wrapped in swaddling cloths and lying in a manger." Mary just smiled at them.

(Incredulous.) I couldn't believe my ears—an *angel* did he say? Then another shepherd said, "He is the promised Savior that Isaiah wrote about. He is Christ the Lord!"

(Pauses again, hardly knowing what to say.) Well! I'm just an ignorant, unschooled woman. What do *I* know? . . . But I have always looked for the promised Messiah. The promise is in all our sacred writings.

(Tries to remember writings.) He is to be born from the line of David, and one of the prophets said that . . . Bethlehem was to be the place. . . . That tiny, innocent baby in our old manger . . . could he be the Messiah? I wonder. . . . I *wonder!*

(After pause, jumps to attention.) Oh . . . oh, my! I've got to go! After I serve the people on the rooftop, I want to bring a hot meal down to the stable. *(Soft, loving expression on her face and in her voice.)* I want to see the baby again! Mary said his name is . . . Jesus. *(Exits hurriedly.)*

Anna

LUKE 2:22-38; ISAIAH 9:6-7

Phanuel—FAN-you-el
Simeon—SIM-ee-un
Caleb—KAY-leb
Gentiles—JEN-tyles
Hebron—HEE-brun
Galilee—GAL-lih-lee

Anna is an old prophetess in the temple in Jerusalem. She lives in the temple, and her life revolves around her worship, prayers, and fasting. She has been a widow for many years.

She is dressed in a long dark robe, with a hood or long scarf draped around her head. She carries herself erect.

The scene is the steps of the temple. Two benches are set back a little from the front of the scene, one to either side, as if they're lining the entrance to the temple.

(Anna is joyful and excited as she comes hurriedly into the scene, pushing a few people aside in her effort to catch up with someone.)

72

Excuse me. . . . Excuse me, please. . . . *(Comes to person she wishes to stop at middle of scene.)*

Excuse me, young woman. . . . Yes, yes, you! . . . *(Breathless.)* Pardon me for chasing after you this way, but I need to talk to you a moment. Do you mind? . . . Oh, thank you. . . . Yes, I'm a little breathless, but I'll be all right. I just wanted to be sure to catch you before you left the temple. . . . I just wanted . . . I just wanted to see your baby.

(Smiles and nods. Reaches out as if to open blanket of baby being held in mother's arms.) Oh, yes, I just wanted to see him . . . and to touch him. *(Reaches out to touch baby.)* What is his name, may I ask? . . . Jesus! Oh, that's a good name. . . . Me? Oh, I am Anna, daughter of Phanuel, of the tribe of Asher. I live here in the temple, worshiping, praying, helping where I can. I've lived here for many, many years, ever since my husband died. I'm known as a prophetess.

(Touches baby.) What a beautiful baby! . . . I couldn't help but hear what happened back there with Simeon when you brought your offerings. . . . I've never seen Simeon so interested in anyone. He often comes to the temple because he's a devout, holy man, but he usually doesn't pay much attention to anyone or anything while he's here. . . .

Yes, I understand that. You came to bring the offerings. . . . What *is* your name, young woman? . . . Mary! . . . Again, I apologize for disturbing you, but . . . but this baby. . . . Simeon said he was the salvation of the Lord, a light for revelation to the Gentiles,

and for glory to the people Israel. That can only mean.
. . .

(Pauses, as if listening.) Yes, I understand. Your visit to the temple was not meant to be for the child, but for Mary's purification. It's been 40 days since he was born. . . .

(Stops them from leaving.) Oh, please . . . before you go . . . may I . . . may I hold the baby for a moment? *(Takes child and holds him on left arm, gently touching him with right hand. Rocks him back and forth.)*

He's beautiful. . . . Look at those eyes, so bright, so alert. . . . Simeon said, "Lord, now lettest thou thy servant depart in peace, according to thy word; for mine eyes have seen thy salvation which thou hast prepared in the presence of all people, a light for revelation to the Gentiles, and for glory to thy people Israel." To think . . . to think that I, old Anna, should see this child, should touch this child. . . .

(Jerks to attention.) Oh, of course . . . here he is. . . . *(Hands baby back.)* I know you'll take *very* good care of him. . . . Goodbye. . . .

(Turns to walk away, then remembers something. Turns back and calls.) Mary! . . . Mary! . . . Where are you from? Where do you live? . . . Oh, they're gone! They've disappeared right into the crowd! I don't know where they live or where they're from. . . . They could be from anywhere! Anyplace! . . . But just imagine! I saw the Lord's salvation—I saw the Messiah!

(Starts calling to people around her.) Benjamin! Da-

vid! Did you see that couple and the baby? That was the Lord's Messiah! Simeon said so, too! He was prophesying just a few moments ago about it! . . . Everyone! Did you hear? We saw the Lord's Messiah, the one who will redeem Israel! . . . It's happened, Caleb, it's happened! The Lord's salvation of Israel! I saw the child! The Messiah! . . . Well, ask Simeon then! It's true!

(Walks to bench. Eases herself down.) Oh, I'm an old woman. . . . I must rest. . . . All this excitement! Who would have thought I'd be chasing after babies today! And telling everyone about the Lord's salvation! . . . Who would have thought?

(Smiles, remembering.) That little baby! . . . He certainly doesn't look like the Messiah some people are waiting for! They want a mighty king, a triumphant warrior to deliver us all from the Romans! They wouldn't be too happy with that sweet little baby, Jesus! . . .

But Simeon said he was the Lord's salvation. . . . And I'm remembering something Isaiah said long ago: "For to us a child is born, to us a son is given; and the government will be upon his shoulder, and his name will be called 'Wonderful Counselor, Mighty God, Everlasting Father, Prince of Peace.' Of the increase of his government and of peace there will be no end, upon the throne of David, and over his kingdom, to establish it, and to uphold it with justice and with righteousness from this time forth and for evermore. The zeal of the Lord of hosts will do this."

It sounds like a lot for a little baby to be and do!

But babies grow up. . . . How I wish I knew where that young couple is from. . . . But perhaps that is also the Lord's will. The child should grow up in freedom, away from curious, prying eyes . . . even old Anna's eyes!

(Sighs deeply, rests, then jerks to attention.) Simeon! . . . Simeon! Over here! . . . Sit down with me, Simeon. I'm resting after all the excitement, and you look as if you could use some rest, too! . . . Simeon, I've never seen you become so excited about anything as you did about that baby! Here that young couple came just for the purification offerings for the mother, and you turned it all into an announcement of the salvation of the Lord! . . .

I know! I know! I felt it, too! There was something about that baby! I agree! It was as if the Lord spoke to me, saying, "This is the special one! This! This is the one you've awaited for so long!" Is that what happened to you, Simeon? . . . You heard the child cry? Oh, I didn't hear that. He was awake but very quiet when I saw him. Was it the cry that alerted you? . . .

(Nods as she listens.) I can understand that. Looking back on it now you probably don't even know for sure. It just happened. But I heard your words, and I saw what you did, Simeon, even if you don't remember it all. That young couple was just presenting their offering of two young pigeons when you came walking in and took the child away from the mother. . . . Everyone just looked at you in amazement! They couldn't understand what you were doing! . . . But then you lifted that little baby up, presenting him to

the Lord, and you said, "Lord, now lettest thou thy servant depart in peace. . . ."

How long have you known that you would not see death until you had seen the Lord's Messiah? . . . Well, it seems the Spirit's revelation has come true. And now you can die, knowing that the Lord is faithful. . . .

That's the way I feel, too, Simeon. I've lived in this temple for so long. It's been more than 60 years—do you realize that? . . . But never have I known the joy and excitement that I've had today! Oh, Simeon, to think that we've been given the privilege of seeing the Messiah. I really can't believe it. . . . Me, old Anna! And you, old Simeon! *(Laughs joyously, teasing Simeon.)*

Ah, yes. . . . Two old people who have been looking and waiting, looking and waiting. . . . And finally we see the Lord's salvation, the Christ, the Messiah. *(Gets up slowly, walks to spot where she held Jesus.)*

I chased them, Simeon, after they left you. . . . Old Anna chased them! And I caught them! I wanted to see that baby. I wanted to hold him. . . . Oh, yes, they were very nice about it. They let me hold him. . . . Right here, right here. *(Pretends to hold baby again.)* Just like this. I held the little Messiah.

(Looks out over audience, over Jerusalem.) Simeon, right here from the steps of the temple we can see Jerusalem. With dusk coming on, the fires and candles are beginning to gleam. . . . I wonder where that young couple and the baby are tonight. They might live here in the city, or they might live south, near Hebron. . . . Or perhaps they live north of here, in

Galilee, or maybe near the sea. Perhaps they're traveling tonight. . . .

They're poor, Simeon, you noticed that, didn't you? . . . Only two pigeons to bring as an offering—no lamb. Yes, they're poor. . . .

No! *(Emphatically.)* No, Simeon, I'm wrong! They're not poor at all. They're rich! They have the Prince of Peace in their arms! . . . I wonder if they know. I wonder if they understand. . . .

(Starts toward exit.) Come, Simeon, it's late. Join me for the evening meal. Tonight we'll give thanks to the Lord of Israel—together! *(Exits.)*

The woman
in the Upper Room

JOHN 3:1-15; 19:38-42; MATTHEW 26:17-35;
MARK 14:12-31; LUKE 22:1-39

Tirzah—TEER-zah
Emmaus—em-MAY-us
Sanhedrin—san-HEE-drin
Arimathea—air-ih-muh-THEE-ah
Nicodemus—nick-uh-DEE-mus
Seder—SAY-dur
aloes—AL-lows

The woman in the Upper Room is imaginary, but
she tells about an extremely important event: the
Last Supper Jesus had with his disciples at which
the Sacrament of Holy Communion was instituted.

The woman, Tirzah, is dressed in a long gown
with a hood. This is meant to represent an outer
garment, a coat. If a coat-like garment is not
available, a shawl can be used.

The drama takes place at night in the home of
an important man in Jerusalem. The woman and
her husband have been brought here in secrecy.

A single wooden bench would be sufficient,
although a table and another bench would add to
the scene.

(Tirzah enters the scene slowly, looking about her in nervousness and fright. She slowly walks to the bench and sits down, all the while looking around, not knowing what's about to happen.)

My name is Tirzah. . . . Yes, that's my husband, David. *(Looks in his direction.)* Yes, thank you, I'm quite comfortable. *(Looks extremely uncomfortable, sitting stiffly.)* No, thank you, I don't want anything to eat.

(Becomes a little bolder.) What I *do* want is an explanation! Here we've been taken from our home at this awful hour of the night and brought here without a word. Everyone has been very kind, but there are rumors flying around Jerusalem that people who have known Jesus are being. . . . *(Covers mouth quickly with hand, realizing she's said too much.)* No, I'm not going to say any more. My husband will do the talking.

(Sits with arms folded and head bowed for a count of five slow beats, then looks up sharply, listening. Speaks loudly.) That's not the way it was, David! Don't you remember. . . . *(Suddenly realizes she's talking again. Covers her mouth.)*

Why are you asking us all these questions? And why did you have us taken from our home in the middle of the night? *(Listens.)* You're not arresting us? . . . You're not the men who put Jesus on trial? . . . Well. . . . *(Reconsidering, glances at husband.)* Well, all right, I'll tell you what I know about the Passover meal.

(Settles herself more comfortably.) First I have to

say that we've known Jesus for quite a while. David and I are followers of Jesus. We really expected to be arrested tonight. Jesus was crucified yesterday, and he's lain in his tomb for a day and a half. His disciples have hidden themselves, and David and I have been very careful, because Jesus spent some of his last hours at our house. We have children, and we don't want to end up in prison or even . . . on a cross.

You must understand! We loved Jesus and we believed his words! But now that he's been crucified as a criminal. . . . Well, it's very dangerous for all of us who knew him and followed him. . . .

But you wanted to know about the Passover meal. . . . We have a large upper room in our house. It's frequently used by groups of people who need space for a banquet or meeting. David and I make part of our living by renting the room and serving the meals. But for Jesus, of course, we gave the room and our services as a gift. . . .

It was rather strange, actually, how Jesus happened to use the room. We often rent it out for feasts, but not too often for Passover meals because families usually prefer to be in their own homes. On the day of Passover my brother was visiting from Emmaus— we were planning to have the Passover meal together. I had sent my brother out to the well to get water and I was busily preparing the bread and meat for our dinner. After a time my brother returned with the water, but to our surprise he had Peter and John with him. . . .

(Listens to someone speaking.) Yes, Peter and John.

. . . Of course I'm sure! We know all Jesus' disciples very well! *(Looks a little disturbed at the interruption; quickly sighs.)*

Anyway . . . as soon as they entered our house they said to David: "The Teacher says to you, Where is the guest room, where I am to eat the Passover with my disciples?" You see, Jesus had never actually used our upper room. But he knew about it, even though he hadn't been in our house. . . . David took Peter and John upstairs and showed them the banquet tables all prepared for a meal. And they took over from there. . . . *(Listens to someone speak.)* No, they did most of the preparations. I helped them but they knew what they wanted and how they wanted it done. . . .

I agreed to serve the meal to Jesus and his disciples. David and my brother and our children and I ate *our* Passover meal a little early. Peter and John had told us that their meal would not start until later in the evening, so we had plenty of time. *(Gets up, wanders about.)*

Everything was ready when they came. All 12 of the disciples accompanied Jesus up the stairs to the upper room and they settled themselves at the tables. I served the wine and the unleavened bread immediately, and then brought the meat and the fruit and the herbs. It was my plan to bring all the food to them, and then give them as much privacy as possible. . . . *(Pauses and indicates hesitation, perhaps by biting lip or chewing fingernail.)*

No. . . . I didn't actually leave them. . . . I felt responsible for the meal—after all, Jesus had come to our house—so I just stayed in the shadows by the far wall and waited and watched. There were several times when I could see they were running short of wine, and one time some food spilled. I took care of those little problems and went back to the shadows. . . .

(Becomes a little upset.) I was *not* intruding! In fact, Jesus knew I was there. . . . How do I know that? Because he spoke to me about it. . . . I was filling the wine cups and Jesus thanked me and said, "Tirzah, I'm glad you're here." *(Looks triumphantly at her questioners. Continues to move about.)*

Well, then I went back to my place in the shadows. They continued to eat the meal and hold the Seder service. Everything was going just the way it was supposed to until . . . until. . . . *(Comes back to bench and slowly seats herself.)*

Toward the end of the meal, Jesus started saying things that weren't in the actual Seder service. I paid special attention because it was so different. Jesus took some of the bread, and blessed it, and broke it, and gave pieces of it to all the disciples. Then he said, "Take, eat; this is my body." I was amazed! What could he mean—this was his body? It was just some of my unleavened bread! I could see the disciples whispering among themselves as if *they* didn't know what he meant either. Then Jesus took a cup of wine. He blessed it and passed it around to all the disciples. He said, "Drink of it, all of you; for this is my blood of the covenant, which is poured out for many for the forgiveness of sins. I tell you I shall not drink again of the fruit of the vine until that day when I drink it new with you in my Father's kingdom."

(Pauses, listening to a question.) I didn't know what it meant. The disciples whispered among themselves again. They continued eating and celebrating the service. I stood in the shadows and thought about Jesus' words. . . .

(Looks toward husband, then back toward questioners.) David wants me to tell you what I told *him* when I came downstairs. . . . The longer I stood there in the shadows, the more apprehensive I became. I kept thinking about Jesus' words: "My blood of the covenant, which is poured out for many." "I shall not drink again of the fruit of the vine." And I found myself in a chill, with my heart just racing. "Jesus is going to die," I said to myself. "Jesus is going to die very soon."

We all knew about the trouble he'd been having with the leaders of the temple and the Sanhedrin, but I never seriously thought that . . . that they would . . . . *(Buries face in hands, then lifts head. Her voice reflects her misery.)* And now we know that Jesus was arrested and tried just hours after he left our upper room. . . . And he's been crucified . . . and he really is *dead!* . . . I keep thinking, "Maybe we could have *done* something to *prevent* it!" *(Her voice gets higher and tighter as she struggles to get control of herself.)*

(Calmly.) I must tell you about something else. . . . *(Gets up and moves about.)* When Jesus said those words over the bread and wine, a word ran through my head: "sacrifice." That's exactly what it sounded

84

like—that Jesus' body and blood would be a sacrifice. How many lambs and bulls have we seen sacrificed in the temple? How often has the blood run and the flesh been offered to God? *(Struggles for words.)* And I thought, "Maybe Jesus himself must be sacrificed so we can live and be free."

(Listens.) I know, I *know!* It doesn't make any sense. . . . But I can't help but remember something the disciple Andrew told us one time. Do you remember this, David? *(Looks toward husband.)* Andrew said that shortly after Jesus had been baptized, John pointed at Jesus and told Andrew, "Behold the Lamb of God." Now, doesn't *that* give you something to think about?

(Pauses, listening to someone speak.) If that's all you want to know, perhaps David and I could go back home. It's very late. . . .

(Suddenly walks to middle of scene, as if confronting someone.) All the time we've been here, I've been trying to think who you are. You look familiar to me, but. . . . *(Suddenly smiles.)* Oh, I'm so happy to meet you at last! Jesus spoke of you. . . . Yes! He did! He mentioned that you had come to him one night and had so many wonderful questions and insights. I know Jesus prayed for you and wanted to visit with you again. . . . You did? Really? David, did you hear that? This man helped Joseph of Arimathea bury Jesus, and he brought myrrh and aloes for the body.

Thank you for telling me. . . . It makes me feel better to know you were there. *(Walks toward doorway.)* Goodnight, Nicodemus! *(Exits.)*

Pilate's wife

MATTHEW 27:1-2, 11-26; LUKE 23:1-25

Pontius—PON-tee-us
Pilate—pilot
Barabbas—buh-RAB-us

Claudia Procula, the name tradition gives to
Pilate's wife, should be dressed in a long robe,
suggesting a dressing gown of rich quality.

The scene is divided, in the imagination, into
two areas: a room on the second floor of the palace,
which has a window overlooking the street; and a
balcony overlooking the judgment hall.

At the end of the drama Claudia Procula will
proceed to a spot designated as the place Pilate
stood during the trial. The actress should decide
ahead of time where these imaginary places are so
she can move smoothly between them.

*(Claudia Procula enters slowly by a side entrance or
side aisle. She walks slowly toward the front, acting
as if she has just awakened—yawning, stretching,
rubbing her eyes and the back of her neck. If acoustics*

permit, she may start speaking a couple lines while she's still walking into the scene.)

Oh, it's so hard to wake up this morning! Those dreams I was having in the middle of the night were so terrible. *(Shudders.)* And now that it's finally morning, I really don't feel rested.

(Looks out imaginary window, perhaps leaning on imaginary sill.) But it's so nice to be in Jerusalem for a change! I love the palace by the sea, but there's so much excitement, so much to see and do in Jerusalem, especially at this time of year. Oh, Passover time— what fun it is! Tonight we'll be entertaining all those guests in the garden room. I'll have to take a nap this afternoon so I can enjoy the evening.

(Cranes neck to see down street.) What's all that commotion down there? What is that crowd of people doing at this early hour? . . . *(Gasps.)* Why, they have Jesus of Nazareth! . . . *(Slowly follows group with eye and head movement.)* What are they *doing?* . . . They're dragging him along the street. . . . And they sound so *angry!* Oh, that poor man! He can hardly walk. . . . What *is* it they're saying? . . . "Blasphemer." "He says he's King of the Jews!" . . . I don't understand this at all!

Oh, they must have made a mistake. That wonderful man has helped so many people. Why are they persecuting him like this? . . . *(Draws sharp breath.)* They're bringing him *here*—to the governor's palace! That means Pontius will have to see them! What is going *on?*

(Turns away from window. Paces a little.) Oh, this

is terrible! Bringing him here means he's going to be tried before Pontius. But what has he *done* to deserve this? Why, I've heard he's healed so many people, and he tells of ways to live in love and mercy. His followers are just humble people from the country. What harm could they have been doing? . . . Oh, this is wrong, very wrong! . . .

(Has idea.) There's that private balcony that overlooks the judgment hall. I'm going to find out what's going on! *(Makes way to imaginary balcony overlooking judgment hall. May walk up and down chancel steps, if scene is being played there.)*

Just look at those people! They're so angry! Yelling and waving their arms! . . . Oh, there's Pontius now, coming to the judgment seat. There—now they're quieting down. Perhaps I can hear what the trouble is. . . .

Oh, my! They're claiming Jesus is harming the nation and forbidding them to give tribute to Caesar. What nonsense that is! And they're saying Jesus claims to be Christ, a king. . . . Jesus doesn't deny being a king. Pontius has asked him several times now. I can't hear his words, but he's not denying it. . . .

There! *Good!* Pontius is telling the crowd he finds no fault in this man. He wants to release him! *(Appears happy and gratified, but her expression soon changes to dismay.)* But the crowd won't have that. They're crying out to *crucify* Jesus! Oh, no. . . . Oh, Pontius—no! You mustn't let them do that! . . .

Now they want Barabbas released from prison. That

criminal! . . . Oh! *(Covers ears with hands and turns away.)* I can't stand the noise!

(Suddenly startled and frightened, gasps and puts hands to her mouth, remembering.) Oh! My dream! . . . It was just like this! . . . The people—and an innocent man! . . . Oh, Pontius, you're going to be caught in the middle of this mess. You mustn't let them take Jesus! It was in my dream! It was in my *dream!*

(Looks around frantically, then beckons to someone.) You! *You!* Come here quickly! . . . Listen carefully! You must bring my husband a message! Now tell him this—"Have nothing to do with that righteous man, for I have suffered much over him today in a dream." Do you understand? Then go quickly—quickly!

(Turns to look over balcony.) Oh, hurry, hurry. Get to him before it's too late. . . . Hurry, hurry! . . . *There!* He got to Pontius. He's talking to him. . . . Oh, Pontius, please, please listen!

(Her attention is drawn to crowd.) I think there's going to be a *riot!* Somebody's going to get hurt! If it's not Jesus it's going to be my husband! Oh, it can't be either one of them! It can't! . . . Pontius is calling for their attention. . . . What's he going to do? . . . He's giving them a *choice* between Jesus and Barabbas! . . . And the people are crying to have *Barabbas* released! This is ridiculous! Just yesterday they were rejoicing because Barabbas was finally in prison! Now they want him released! . . .

Pontius is speaking again. . . . I can hardly hear him for the noise. . . . What is he saying? . . . "Then what

89

. . . shall I . . . do . . . with Jesus . . . who is called Christ?"

(Puts hands over ears and turns away.) Oh, no, no, no! They want Jesus *crucified!* That's a death only for the very lowest, the very worst of criminals! *(Takes hands from ears, but still does not look at crowd.)* And this gentle man of God—indeed, he may be the son of God—*crucified!* I can't *bear* it!

(Turns reluctantly, slowly back to look over balcony.) Now what, *now* what? . . . Pontius is calling for something from the servants. . . . What is it? . . . Oh, it's *water* in a silver basin. . . . And he's washing his hands in the water. . . . Oh, I know what he's doing— he's ridding himself of the guilt of this act. . . . There —he just said so: "I am innocent of this man's blood; see to it yourselves." And the crowd is crying that the blood will be on them and their children. . . . *(Sad.)* Oh, Pontius, if only it were that simple! What have you done, what have you done?

(Watches crowd and Pilate move.) There goes Pontius back into the palace. . . . And the soldiers and the people are taking Jesus away. *(Pauses a moment, then sighs deeply.)*

How quiet it is all of a sudden. The silence is so sad. . . . They left the water in the basin down there. . . . I'm going to go get it. *(Slowly moves to spot she has been looking at during drama. Picks up imaginary basin and faces audience.)*

Water—it's just water. . . . I heard once sometime ago that John called the Baptist was baptizing people in the water of the Jordan River. And that Jesus was baptized by John. . . . And I heard that Jesus once turned water into wine at a wedding. . . . Another time they say that Jesus walked on the water to reach his disciples in a boat. . . . And now . . . he's delivered to be crucified . . . with *water*.

Oh, Pontius, you think you're finished with this man called Jesus, but you're not. . . . None of us ever will be. *(Exits slowly, preferably down aisle to back of church or room, carrying imaginary basin.)*

Peter's wife

LUKE 22:14-71; MATTHEW 16:13-23; JOHN 16

Mara—MAR-ah
Galilee—GAL-lih-lee
Sanhedrin—san-HEE-drin

Peter's wife, Mara, is a young woman, rather small and slender. She wears a long gown, caught at the waist, of ordinary fabric and color.

The scene is Peter's home in Jerusalem. A table and two benches are arranged for eating.

Mara's voice and mood change during the drama. At first she is a concerned and sweet wife, but gradually she becomes stronger and stronger in her words and convictions, momentarily taking charge of her big husband. Then she calms down again and is stunned by her own strength and courage.

(Mara comes hurriedly into the scene and stands watching her husband pace back and forth. Her head moves to indicate his movement as she talks to him.)
Peter, please, I beg you, please come and lie down.

I will bring you some wine—perhaps that will make you sleep. *(Anxiously watches him pace.)*

Peter, you have been pacing like this for hours. You must be *exhausted!* Look outside—the sun is shining! You haven't slept at all! . . . Neither have I!

All right . . . just sit down. Sit down here at the table. You've been talking and mumbling all night, but I really haven't been able to make much sense out of it. Try to tell me what has happened. . . . *I know* it's terrible! I *know* Jesus has been arrested and is on trial. You've told me all that. What I don't understand is why you're cursing yourself. . . .

Peter, I'm frightened! I've never heard you talk like this. Not even before you knew Jesus did you *ever* speak like this. . . . *Please* tell me what's wrong. Maybe you'll feel better if you can just talk about it.

(Pauses, listening to him speak.) I *promise* I won't hate you. Peter, I *love* you! I've become used to the impulsive things you say and do, but I can't bear seeing you suffer like this. . . .

(Sits on one bench and motions to other.) Come now . . . sit down so we can talk. . . . Good, good. . . . Now, Peter, what has happened that's so terrible? *(Listens for a moment, then her face tightens in emotion. Puts hands to her mouth.)* Oh, no! Oh, no! . . . I understand, yes, I understand. . . . No, no, I don't hate you. I don't hate you at all. . . . Oh, I just *hurt* so for you. . . . *(Gets up to pace.)*

Now where did all this happen, Peter? . . . In the courtyard of the high priest's house. I see. . . . And there were a lot of people there, and some of them

93

recognized you, is that it? . . . And you told them that you didn't know Jesus. . . . Did you feel it was dangerous, Peter? Were you afraid of being arrested yourself? . . . *(Nods.)* I understand, I understand.

(Comes back to table and sits on her bench.) But what do you mean by "the cock was crowing"? I don't understand why that's important. The cocks crow every morning. . . . Oh, I see. . . . Jesus had told you that you would deny him three times before the cock crowed. . . . *Three times,* Peter? . . . Three times. . . . And then the cock crowed. . . .

(Leans across table to reach toward Peter.) Peter! You still haven't told me the whole story. . . . I can tell. . . . *(Listens for a moment.)* Of course it hurt! . . . Jesus looked right at you when the cock crowed. . . . Like a sword going through your heart. . . . I'm sure it was. . . . And then? . . . And then you ran away, weeping.

(Gets up to pace.) Go ahead, let the tears come. There has to be cleansing before there can be healing. . . . Of course there'll be healing. You talk as if everything is over. . . . No, I'm sorry, I don't agree.

Yes, you denied Jesus, and that was wrong. You know that. But what you're saying is that Jesus will not love you anymore, that he won't forgive you. And we both know that is not true. . . . Why, Peter! You told me that Jesus has prayed for you. *Remember what he said!* . . . Then listen to *me* say it! You told me his words and they're just what you need to be thinking about now: "Simon, Simon, behold, Satan demanded to have you that he might sift you like wheat, but I have prayed for you that your faith may not fail; and when you have turned again, strengthen your brethren." Peter! Jesus prayed that your faith may not fail. But look at you! . . .

(*Leans over him, hands on hips.*) Oh, Satan must be laughing for joy! He's got you right where he wants you, Simon Peter! He's sifting you like wheat and breaking you up into tiny pieces. Where's that strong fisherman Jesus called at the Sea of Galilee? Where's the man who confessed that he believed Jesus was the Christ? Where's the disciple who saw Jesus transfigured on the mountain and wanted to build booths?

(*Paces, sighing in exasperation.*) Do you really think this is the end of the line for you? With all the promises Jesus has made regarding the work of the kingdom and how his followers will be empowered to do it? . . . Think now! Think! Jesus has been telling you for a long time that he would suffer and die! . . . Yes, things look very bad for him now. The leaders of the Sanhedrin have him in their power, and let's face it, Peter—Jesus will probably die. They've been wanting to destroy him for a long time. But he's been *telling* you that. His suffering and death should come as no surprise to you. What do you think Jesus has been preparing you for, you and Andrew and John and James and all the rest? To fall apart when everything looks grim? To cave in when the going gets rough? . . . I don't believe it!

(*Paces, working off her anger, then stops to listen to Peter. Comes back to table and sits down, in control of herself.*)

Say that again, Peter. . . . Jesus told you that tonight?
. . . Don't you see? That proves what I've been telling
you. Jesus will send his Spirit, the Counselor, to
strengthen you. He knows he must die. He knows he
must leave you, but he is not deserting you. . . .

Now there you go again, feeling so sorry for Simon
Peter! Remember Jesus' words: "When you have
turned again, strengthen your brothers." Jesus knew
you would be weak tonight and deny him. He knows
you very well, my husband! Blazing with enthusiasm
one moment and cringing with fear the next. But he
is counting on you to help the others. "When you have
turned again, strengthen your brethren," Simon Peter!
This is the time to ask God's forgiveness and to help
the other disciples. That is what Jesus wants you to
do. . . .

*(Bows head and folds hands in prayer, counting five
slow beats.)* Blessed be the God of Israel. . . .

*(Her voice is calm. The mood is much more re-
laxed.)* Peter. . . . It is Friday, and the sun is already
high in the heavens. I know you cannot sleep and that
you want to find Andrew and the rest of the men.
But please eat something before you leave. This will
be a very long and difficult day, I'm sure of that. . . .

*(Stands up and goes to side of scene opposite door-
way, thinking her own thoughts. The imaginary Peter
is eating at the table. She gazes out over audience.)*
How could I say all those things to him? I, Mara, who
am known as "Peter's wife," who stands in his shadow
most of the time—where did I get the strength to say
such stern words? . . . Ah, yes, from you, O Lord of

Israel! You gave me the words to speak and the courage to say them. . . .

O Lord, we believe that Jesus is your Chosen One, your Servant. The dark clouds of trouble have been gathering about him, and it would seem that today the Sanhedrin will have its way. O Lord, if Jesus dies, that will mean trouble and persecution for all his followers. Peter might have denied that he knew Jesus last night in the darkness, but in the bright light of day everyone knows he's the big fisherman from Galilee, a disciple of Jesus.

(Glances back at table.) Peter has eaten his meal and now he's gone. He will go first to find his brother Andrew, I'm sure. And then. . . . O Lord, you gave me the strength to speak your words to Peter. Now fill him with your strength, that he may do what is needful today, and may not falter in his faith.

(Walks to doorway and looks out.) Look at that! The sun was shining so brightly before, and now it's getting darker and darker. And I don't see rain clouds either. . . . *(Walks slowly back into scene, hugs herself, shivers.)* There's such an ominous feeling in the air. And that darkness! . . .

(Suddenly grabs table and hangs on, acts out the shaking of earthquake.) Oh! . . . The earth is moving. . . . It's an earthquake! . . . Oh, it's rumbling and shaking! . . . Oh, God of Israel, help me! . . .

(Now stands firm. Quake is over. Relaxes and looks toward doorway. There's a long pause as realization dawns on her.) The Chosen One . . . is dead. *(Slowly exits.)*

Mary, mother of Jesus (II)

(At the foot of the cross)
MATTHEW 27:32-56; MARK 15:16-41;
LUKE 1:26-38; 2:22-35; 23:26-49;
JOHN 19:17-37; 8:12

Golgotha—GALL-guh-thah
centurion—sen-TOUR-ee-un
Simeon—SIM-ee-un
Gentiles—JEN-tyles
Jacob—JAY-cup

Mary is a middle-aged woman dressed in a dark robe. She has a hood or dark shawl over her head.

There is no furniture in the scene; it is bare. Mary stands just a short way from the cross on which Jesus is crucified. The imaginary cross is in the audience, so Mary faces the people, looking upward, to look at Jesus on the cross. She is near the middle of the scene. She moves about occasionally, but usually remains quite still, sometimes looking up at Jesus, often looking straight ahead or closing her eyes.

Mary is in the company of several imaginary people, with whom she speaks. But it's her inward thoughts that she is revealing.

She is emotional, but not weeping. She is in

98

control, but it's with obvious effort. She feels she should be here, even though it's painful for her. She believes her presence will comfort her son.

(Mary enters quietly. She speaks in a controlled way, but her voice is tight and sad.)

No, please, I must stay here. *(Resists people trying to lead her away.)* I must stay here. *(Looks up at cross.)* There are moments when I think he looks down and sees me. I think perhaps it comforts him a little. Of course I'm tired, but it makes no difference how *I* feel at this moment. All that matters is that he knows we are here . . . and that we love him so much that we're not afraid to be here. . . .

Those soldiers will not hurt us. They've crucified their prisoners and nothing can be done to change that. We are no threat to them. They know we are helpless against their weapons.

(Looks around.) What a gloomy, sad place this is. Golgotha it's called—the place of the skull. The rocks on the far side of this hill look like a skull, a mask of death. No wonder they crucify their prisoners here— the place *reeks* of death.

(Sighs deeply, looks at sky.) Have you noticed how dark it is? When we came this morning the sun was shining, but now the sky has turned black. It looks like it should storm, but there aren't any rain clouds in the sky. It's just dark: dark like I feel inside; dark as if it's the end of the world; dark as . . . death. . . .

Do you remember? Jesus once said, "I am the light of the world; he who follows me will not walk in darkness, but will have the light of life." Now that he is dying, it is getting darker and darker.

(Looks at cross, is quiet for a moment, then speaks to person with her with great emotion.) I cannot believe that is my son on that cross! . . . What has he done to deserve this? Nothing! Nothing but heal people and teach them and feed them and love them. . . . Listen to him groan! Such pain as he must be having! . . . Oh, I pray that he'll die soon. He's been hanging there five hours. . . .

(Looks up quickly, with attention.) I think he's trying to speak to us! Listen, listen. . . . *(Concentrates, trying to hear. After a moment, turns to look at person next to her, then looks back to cross, then back to person.)* John, he spoke to me: "Woman, behold your son." And then he spoke to you: "Behold, your mother." Jesus gave us into each other's care, John. . . .

Yes, I love you, too. You will be my son now. . . . No, no, please! We must wait, John. I'm all right. I can't leave yet. The time won't be long, I'm sure of that. . . . He must be very close to death.

(Looks at cross.) He's speaking again. *(Concentrates, looking upward.)* Ohh. . . . *(Moans softly with hand to mouth, then turns to John.)* Did you hear that? He said, "My God, my God, why hast thou forsaken me." Oh, he must feel so abandoned, and we are so helpless. . . .

Jesus has always had such a special relationship with God. Even when he was little he spoke so freely and confidently of "his Father," and we all knew he was not speaking about Joseph. Once when Jesus was about

12 years old we lost him in the crowds of people at the festival in Jerusalem. It took us three days to locate him, and there he was in the temple, asking questions and listening to the rabbis teach. When I scolded him for making us worry, he looked at me with such innocent puzzlement and said, "How is it that you searched for me? Did you not know that I must be in my Father's house?"

(Looks up at cross.) He spoke again, John. I couldn't hear what he said. . . . Yes, you're right! He must have said he was thirsty. They're offering him something to drink from a sponge. See how they've put the sponge on a stick and are putting it near his mouth. . . . He's taking some . . . but now he's turning away. Oh, John, he's getting much weaker. . . .

Listen! *(Listens attentively.)* "It is finished," he said. What does that mean, I wonder. . . . His life is almost over, so *that* is finished. . . . His work of healing and teaching is certainly over. . . . What do *you* think it means, John? . . . Yes, perhaps that's it: The work his Father sent him to do is completed. *(In anguish.)* But I don't understand any of it, John! . . .

(Listens, looking up, then puts both hands to her face, close to weeping.) Oh . . . oh, I think . . . I think it really is finished now. He prayed to his Father, giving his spirit up to him, and now, look! . . . He's limp and not moving. . . .

(Calls out loudly, in great sorrow.) Is he dead? . . . Is my son dead? . . . *(Her head and shoulders droop.)* Yes, my son is dead. He is with his Father. . . . Blessed be the name of the Lord.

(Covers her face and weeps, but is jerked into reality. Acts out rolling of earthquake. Leans quickly from side to side, trying to balance, then holding her hands out. Cries out in fright.) John! What is it? What's happening? . . . An earthquake! When Jesus died . . . an earthquake! *(Looks around.)* Look over there . . . *(Points.)* Those boulders, those huge boulders are split! . . . Oh, God is telling us of his anger and sorrow! . . . I can still feel the earth rumbling! . . .

John, did you hear that! Look at the centurion by the cross! I heard him say, "Truly, this was a son of God!" Even this Roman soldier believes Jesus was from God.

(Walks slowly to side, then stops to look back.) John, when we took Jesus to the temple to present my purification offerings, when he was 40 days old, an old prophet named Simeon was there. He said that it had been revealed to him that he should not see death before he had seen the Christ. He got so excited when he saw Jesus! He took Jesus into his arms and prayed to God, blessing and praising the Lord. He described Jesus as the salvation of God, and said he'd be a light for revelation to the Gentiles, and a glory to Israel.

But he said something to me, John, that I've never forgotten. He said, "Behold, this child is set for the fall and rising of many in Israel, and for a sign that is spoken against, that thoughts out of many hearts may be revealed."

And he said something else, especially to me, John. He said that all this would mean that "a sword will pierce through your own soul also." I've never quite known what that meant . . . until today. My soul is indeed pierced . . . with sorrow, with anger, with fear, with confusion, with more unhappiness than I could have imagined. . . . "A sword will pierce through your own soul also," the prophet said. Today the sword found its mark, John. . . .

(Looks back at cross.) They have pierced his side, John, the blood and water have come out. I have been pierced too, and all my sorrow and misery are pouring out. . . .

(Turns to go, sighs deeply; moves a few more steps out of scene if there's room.) But, John . . . I just remembered something else! *(Becomes animated and hopeful.)* When the angel first announced to me that Jesus would be born, and that he would be the Son of the Most High, he described Jesus as a king, and he described his kingdom as having no end. . . . The words? Well, the angel said, "He will be great, and will be called the Son of the Most High; and the Lord God will give to him the throne of his father David, and he will reign over the house of Jacob for ever; and of his kingdom there will be no end."

It does seem strange, doesn't it. He's to be a king over a kingdom with no end, he will reign forever. . . . *(Points to cross.)* But there he hangs on a cross, having just died a criminal's death.

(Shakes head in sorrow and puzzlement.) It doesn't make sense. . . . It doesn't make any sense. . . . *(Covers face and weeps, then drops hands, takes a deep breath, and straightens shoulders.)*

John, I cannot believe that the Lord of Israel has

abandoned his son. I've seen and heard too much before Jesus was born and during his life to believe that. It's completely hidden from me, but there must be a reason for all this—there *must be*. . . . I cannot imagine what the reason is, John. I just know. . . . *(Looks again at cross.)* I just know that Jesus had a special relationship with his Father, the God of Israel, and our God is faithful. He keeps his promises. It was promised to me that Jesus would reign over the house of Jacob forever and there would be no end to his kingdom. . . . Beyond that, I cannot explain or understand. . . .

John . . . take me home. *(Exits slowly.)*

Mary Magdalene

LUKE 8:1-3; JOHN 19:25; 20:1-18

Arimathea—air-ih-muh-THEE-ah
Magdala—MAG-duh-lah
Magdalene—MAG-duh-leen
Galilee—GAL-lih-lee
Pharisees—FAIR-ih-sees
Capernaum—cuh-PER-nah-um

Mary Magdalene is dressed in a rich, long, flowing gown.
She moves gracefully, shows deep emotion.

(Mary Magdalene enters, gazing into the distance, remembering.)

The morning air was very cool, I remember, when I left the house in Jerusalem with my spices. Several of us women had decided on Friday that we would anoint the body of Jesus with the burial spices at the very first opportunity, and I had been careful to notice exactly where Joseph of Arimathea had buried Jesus. It was a new tomb hewn out of rock, close to the place where Jesus had died on the cross.

We would have anointed his body right away, you

105

understand, but it was almost sundown on Friday, and that's the beginning of the Sabbath. No work of any sort is allowed on the Sabbath. So it was very early on the first day of the week before I was finally able to go to the tomb.

(Rubs her arms as if to warm herself.) Yes, it was cool. I wrapped my cloak tightly about me, protecting myself *and* the precious spices. I had waited for the other women to come, but finally I couldn't bear to wait any longer. I left the city gates and began to travel the road that Jesus had traveled a few days earlier. Only . . . he had been dragging that heavy cross, and he had been so very tired.

That Friday was the worst, the very worst day of my life. Some people might say that I, Mary of Magdala, must have had worse days than *that* one, since I've been so ill so much of my life, but if they said that, they'd be wrong. That Friday was the worst. It was on that day that the Son of God died a criminal's death on an ugly cross.

(Her face softens.) Jesus was so special to me. He had shown me how very much God loves me, and he taught me how to love other people. He made it so easy! All I had to do was see the love shining out of *his* face and eyes, and then I could love others too.

My life wasn't always spent showing love to other people. Hardly! I look back now on my former life and it's like thinking about another person. Before I was concerned only for myself—now my concern is for others! Before I worried constantly—now I've learned to trust God in all things! Before I used God's name in vain—now I praise his name at every opportunity! Before I was sick—now I am well! Before I was lost—now I am found!

Does all that sound incredible to you? Imagine how *I* have felt! Jesus turned my life completely around. Now I'm *facing* God instead of running away from him!

(Her mood changes as she remembers illness and pain.) Yes, I was very ill. The physicians in Magdala just shook their heads when they examined me. One doctor said my illness was in my imagination. Another said I had an incurable disease. Still another sadly pulled at his beard and said nothing. Although I possessed great wealth, it was not possible for me to purchase health.

It is difficult to describe how I felt during those years I was ill. Part of the time I'd feel as if I had a high fever, and I would see things that weren't there. Other times I'd feel dizzy, confused, and my words would come out all wrong. Then sometimes I would just feel very, very unhappy. Occasionally I'd experience a time when all I wished to do was sleep. Other times I couldn't sleep at all. I would wander about my beautiful house, which overlooked the Sea of Galilee, and I would ponder my fate in life. How was it that I, Mary Magdalene, with wealth, property, servants, and power, could find no enjoyment from life—and no peace?

(Becomes happily animated.) Peace! And love! Those were the things I noticed first about Jesus! I saw him one evening when I ventured from my house to walk along the Sea of Galilee. I rarely did that, but

the sea was so inviting that evening, and I was feeling so confused and unhappy. So I walked along the pebbly beach, alone as usual. My friends had long ago deserted me. Some Pharisees in Magdala said my illness was caused by demons, and there's nothing like being possessed by demons to drive friends away!

I don't remember exactly what I was thinking, but I do remember that I had stooped to pick up a pretty stone. *(Holds up imaginary stone, examining it.)* I was studying it, noticing the pink coloration, when a quiet voice interrupted my thoughts. "You are Mary," the voice said.

I was startled! Who was this? A friend come back? But no—it was a young man, about 30 years of age, with an expression in his eyes I had never seen before. It was that love and peace I was telling you about!

"Yes," I stammered, "yes, I'm Mary—of Magdala."

"You're not well, Mary," the young man said. "You've suffered for many years."

The expression on my face must have been very strange. I didn't understand how he could know about me. He was a total stranger. I could tell by the way he spoke that he came from south of Magdala. And yet . . . he had approached me from the direction of Capernaum, to the north. I wondered who he could be.

One of the men who accompanied him was a fisherman named Peter from Capernaum. Peter solved the puzzle for me. "This is Jesus of Nazareth," he said. "Andrew and I go with him as he teaches the people about the ways of God."

Suddenly I realized who this was! One of my servant girls had talked about this Jesus! She said she had heard him tell about the . . . kingdom of heaven, and she also said she had seen him . . . heal a leper!

(Confiding in the audience.) I must be honest with you. I didn't care a denarius about any kingdom of heaven. All I could think was, "Maybe he can cure *me!*" It must have shown on my face, because Jesus gently took my two hands in his, and he lifted his face toward the sky. "Father," he said, "Mary is very ill. She has struggled with her illness for many years." Then Jesus looked straight at me. His eyes pierced my very soul! His voice became hard and authoritative. "I command you demons, depart from her!"

(Clutches abdomen, looks stricken.) What I felt then is beyond description! My insides seemed to be fighting a battle, and all I could do was wait for something to win. My legs would not support me, and I slumped to the ground. Suddenly a wild scream came from my throat, but I had no sensation of having made the sound myself. . . .

When the eerie noise stopped, the battle inside me stopped, too. I lay quietly on the beach. I was exhausted, but also . . . completely at peace. It was a brand new feeling for me!

Jesus and Peter helped me to my feet, and I felt strength surging back into me. My thanks to Jesus seemed so inadequate—how do you thank someone for giving your life back to you?

I invited them all to my house for a meal. During that long night Jesus told me how to fill my empty life with the things of the kingdom of heaven. He explained so much to me—things I later heard him teach to many people.

(Smiling and happy.) My whole reason for living changed that night! I decided to use my wealth to help the poor. I often traveled with Jesus as he went from town to town, teaching and healing people. I was there when he rode triumphantly into Jerusalem, when the people shouted "Hosanna!" I shouted, too! . . . And I was there when he was on trial. . . . And finally, I was at the foot of Golgotha hill when he was crucified, and when he died. . . .

I went with Joseph of Arimathea and Nicodemus to see where Jesus would be buried. And then I went to the tomb the first day of the week. . . . *(Pauses, catching herself repeating her words.)* But that's where I began, isn't it? I was telling you how cool it was that morning. . . .

When I reached the tomb, I was amazed! The huge stone that had covered the opening of the grave had been rolled away. The doorway was wide open.

I'll admit it—I was very frightened! I ran all the way back to Jerusalem to get Peter, and soon Peter and John were traveling the road to the grave. Believe me—I wasn't far behind! John arrived first, but Peter was the braver, and he rushed right into the tomb. And, of course, it was *empty!*

Peter and John were baffled—what could have happened? John said several times that Jesus must be alive, but Peter looked like a man in shock. Before long they both headed back to Jerusalem. *(Upset.)* But I couldn't leave. I was weeping because I was frightened and because the body of Jesus was gone. . . . My whole world was once again in shreds.

Then I stooped to look into the tomb, and there were two bright angels, sitting where the body of Jesus had lain. "Woman, why are you weeping?" one of them asked.

"Because they've taken away my Lord, and I do not know where they have laid him," I cried.

I was confused. I turned to go back to Jerusalem. Suddenly I saw a man standing in the little garden outside the tomb. "Woman, why are you weeping? Whom do you seek?" he said. His voice was gentle. My hopes began to rise a little, since I thought he must be the gardener. Surely he must know something that would help me!

(More hopeful.) "Sir, if you've carried him away, tell me where you've laid him, and I will take care of him." But the man just looked at me. Then he said, "Mary."

(Full of wonderment and joy.) In a flash I knew it was Jesus—alive, radiant, *looking* at me! Can I explain to you what I felt? I doubt it! My moment of healing had been extraordinary, and my journeys with Jesus had been inspiring. But this moment when I realized that Jesus had risen from the dead—that was the most beautiful moment in my life.

"Teacher!" I said, and I reached to touch him. But he wouldn't let me do that. Instead he gave me a message for the disciples. I was to tell them that Jesus was ascending to his Father.

(*Animated and joyful.*) If the morning was still cool, I didn't know it anymore! I ran all the way back to Jerusalem, my fourth trip that day!

When I found Peter and John and the rest of the disciples, I cried, "I have seen the Lord! I have seen the Lord!"

And that's what I tell everyone I meet, even now! That's what I'm telling you today! "I have seen the Lord! He is *alive!*" (*Exits joyfully.*)

Zacchaeus' wife

LUKE 19:1-10

Zacchaeus—zuh-KEE-us
Hadassah—ha-DAH-suh
Bartimaeus—bar-tih-MEE-us

Zacchaeus' wife is an energetic person. She wears
an ordinary gown, long and flowing, preferably
violet or purple.

A high stool is placed at center stage.

*(Zacchaeus' wife comes running or walking quickly
down one of the aisles, calling for her friend.)* Hadassah! . . . Hadassah, are you home? . . . Where can she
be anyway? I wish I could find her. . . . Hadassah! . . .

*(Comes to top step of chancel or stage. Looks
around.)* Hadaaaaaasah! . . . Oh, *there* you are! Oh,
I'm so glad I found you—I just *have* to *talk* to you!
. . . Oh, thank you, I will sit down. *(Perches on stool.)*

I'm tired, Hadassah, really *tired*. We've had so much
company in the last couple days. . . . Yes, *us* . . . company! It's such a turnaround, you know. Not many
people have cared to visit at *our* house!

But didn't you hear what happened to Zacchaeus, Hadassah? . . . I mean, *everyone* in Jericho knows about Zacchaeus! . . . Oh, that's right—I remember now! You went to Jerusalem to visit your sister! You weren't even here, were you? . . . Oh, Hadassah, have I got a story to tell *you!*

Well, it was four days ago. Nothing extraordinary about the day at all, Hadassah, just another day after the Sabbath. I had planned to dye some cloth that morning, and Zacchaeus left early to collect taxes on the other side of Jericho. Well, toward noon time I decided to walk to the marketplace to find more dye for my cloth—I'm so tired of purple, Hadassah, I can hardly stand it! *(Plucks at her gown, if it's violet or purple.)*

I was just poking around the market stalls when I heard this commotion around the corner. Well, everyone was going to see what was happening, so I followed them. It seems that Jesus from Nazareth, the carpenter we've heard so much about, had stopped at the well on his way through town. . . . Yes, Hadassah, Jesus was here! Quite a crowd gathered around him. Everyone had heard about the wonderful things he's done—healing the sick, multiplying the loaves of bread, and all the marvelous stories he tells. And, Hadassah, we heard later that he healed old Bartimaeus, the blind beggar, just outside of Jericho the very day he was here!

Naturally I was very curious. I wanted to actually see Jesus, hear him speak. So I was jostling my way through the crowd, trying to peer over all the people. *(Demonstrates her actions.)*

And *then,* Hadassah . . . oh, you're never going to believe this! . . . There was the worst racket on the other side of the crowd. Someone was hollering to let him through, and others were hollering that they wouldn't budge, and there was a great pushing and shoving match for a while. All of a sudden it stopped, and *then* I saw Zacchaeus! . . . Yes, Zacchaeus! He was trying to see Jesus! And the people wouldn't let him through, even though he is so short. They weren't about to do any favors for Zacchaeus—you know how popular he is in Jericho!

But you've got to hand it to Zacchaeus, Hadassah; he's very quick and very clever. People sometimes make the mistake of underrating him just because he isn't very tall, but they should never do that. He'll get around them every time! When he realized he wasn't going to get through the crowd, he thought of another way to see Jesus. He headed straight for that huge, old sycamore tree in the market square and scrambled right up into the branches! There he had a ringside seat! He could see everything, including Jesus. I could see him laughing to himself about how he'd outfoxed everybody again.

Then Jesus got up and started on his way. The crowd milled around him and followed him, and then I realized that Jesus was headed straight for that syca- more tree. Oh, Hadassah, my heart almost stopped! What was this great teacher going to think of that little man up in the tree? *(Looks up, showing conster-nation.)*

Well, if you want to know the truth, Hadassah, I was almost ill when I saw what happened next. Jesus stopped under the tree and called up to Zacchaeus—who wasn't laughing anymore, by the way. I wasn't close enough to hear what Jesus said to him, but soon I heard the crowd mumbling, "What's the matter with Jesus? Why is he associating with the likes of that tax collector? That Zacchaeus is an awful sinner, and there they go off together."

And, Hadassah, they *were* going off together! Zacchaeus had climbed down from the tree, and he and Jesus were heading toward our house! I saw a friend of mine who had been right near Jesus, and I asked her what Jesus had said to my husband. She told me Jesus asked Zacchaeus to come down because he want-ed to stay at his house.

Oh, Hadassah, I've never moved so fast in my life! I took the shortcut through the back field, trying to get home before Zacchaeus and Jesus got there. All the time I was running I was thinking *(breathless)*, "What shall I feed him? Where will he sit? How shall I act? What will the servants say?"

I was so out of breath when I got there I could hard-ly speak, but it wasn't long before I got those servants working. We started roasting meat, cutting vegetables, straightening the furniture, baking bread—Hadassah, you should have seen the commotion!

And then . . . Jesus came! He was so kind to us all, Hadassah. The servants washed his dusty feet, and I brought him a lovely robe to wear. The children gathered around him, and their eyes were just huge! Zacchaeus was a wonderful host. He and Jesus talked a lot before the meal, and afterward too. I could hear them talking about tax collecting and about being honest and living a God-fearing life. I chewed off all my fingernails just listening to that conversation, because *you* know and *I* know and all *Jericho* knows that Zacchaeus has not been fair or honest with his tax collecting. And, Hadassah, he's always been so proud of the way he could collect more taxes than anyone else!

I was afraid of what Jesus would think when Zacchaeus bragged about his tax collecting to *him*. But it was a *miracle,* Hadassah! Zacchaeus hung his head and actually wept—*wept!* He told Jesus how sorry he was, and how he realized now that it was a great sin against God and against the people of Jericho.

And then *another* miracle happened! Zacchaeus promised to give half his riches to the poor, and besides that he promised to multiply by four what he owed to any man. He promised Jesus he wouldn't cheat any more.

Jesus smiled and nodded. He never said a harsh word to Zacchaeus, not one. Just all that love and understanding.

And Zacchaeus has been as good as his word, Hadassah! That's why we've had so much company. People are coming in left and right to tell us how grateful they are. Some of them have brought us little gifts.

(Thoughtful.) You want to know something else,

Hadassah? Zacchaeus wasn't the only one who had a change of heart that day. No . . . no. I felt it, too. I've always felt as if I was a notch above most of the people in Jericho—after all, my husband was wealthy! I loved my beautiful clothes and jewelry. But I see now that was wrong. I should have been caring more for my family and for my neighbors and friends. I feel like a new person, Hadassah, I really do. I feel as if I've been . . . *freed* from a prison—a prison of selfishness! . . .

(Hops down from stool.) I've got to run, Hadassah! I promised the servants the afternoon off. I must go home and send them on their way. Come see me later and I'll tell you about some of the other things Jesus said! . . . Bye now! *(Walks quickly back down the aisle.)*

Mary and Martha

LUKE 10:38-42; JOHN 11:1-45; 12:1-11

Alexandria—al-eck-ZAND-ree-ah
Bethany—BETH-ah-nee
Lazarus—LAZ-uh-rus
pomegranates—POM-eh-gran-its

Mary and Martha both appear in this drama,
but they do not speak to each other. The illusion
to be created is that they are each alone and
thinking their own thoughts. They speak
alternately, but only to voice thoughts, not to
communicate with each other.

Two high stools are set in the middle of the
stage area, about two feet apart, side by side.
An invisible line divides the scene into Mary's
half and Martha's half.

The sisters do not look at each other. If they
happen to glance into the other half of the scene,
it is with unseeing eyes, not focusing.

The middle-aged women are dressed similarly in
long robes, but Martha's dress should be more
ordinary and practical, perhaps of a darker color.
Mary's dress can be brighter. However, neither
robe is of a rich quality. These are average women
in average clothes.

(Mary and Martha enter at the same time, but from opposite sides, going directly to their individual stools to sit down. They remain seated during the entire drama.

Martha looks disgusted and exasperated as she begins speaking. Mary is smiling happily as she quietly sits before her turn to speak.)

Martha: She did it again! My dreamy sister left me with all the housework and cooking again! I thought we had settled that problem. We decided who would do what when we had company, but it seems Mary just forgets those things when the company actually arrives! Like today . . . we had special guests from Jerusalem, a man and woman who have lived in Alexandria, Egypt, for many years. Now, I agree—they were very interesting people! That's part of the reason we invited them to our home here in Bethany. We wanted to hear about Egypt and about the growth of the church there. But what happens? As soon as they come to the door, Mary forgets all about helping me prepare the meat, sweet yams, pomegranates, olives, bread—and she settles down to ask them questions and listen to all their stories. I would have liked to hear the stories, too, but *somebody* had to roast the lamb and prepare the yams and olives and pomegranates! Oh, I can't tell you how disgusted I was!

Mary: This was *such* an exciting day! I can't remember when I've enjoyed two people more than the couple who visited us today. They've recently come to Jerusalem from Alexandria in Egypt, and they have so many stories to tell and ideas to share! For instance, they were telling us that there are many people in Alexandria who have been baptized in Jesus' name! Imagine! There's a church of Jesus in that faraway place! We've heard that this is happening—there apparently are churches in Greece and in Asia Minor, too. It just seems so incredible to me that the news about Jesus and his death and resurrection have spread that far. But it's so *wonderful!* I just can't get enough of the news—I find myself sitting and staring at people who tell me about it!

(Sighs and looks unhappy.) But I'm afraid I made my sister unhappy today. When I think about it, I realize full well that I left her with all the cooking again. I didn't even realize I was neglecting my share of the work. And we had an agreement, too, about how the work would be handled when guests arrived. *(Sighs deeply.)* I'm always so torn—I want to help my sister, but I also want to hear about new ideas. I want to learn from people who can teach me. I remember one time when Jesus was visiting us, something like this happened. . . .

Martha *(still exasperated):* And this isn't the first time Mary has left me with the work when we had important guests! Once when Jesus came to our home the very same thing happened! I was working hard over the meal and serving it, not having a chance to hear Jesus speak . . . and my sister Mary was sitting right at Jesus' feet, listening to every word he said! She knew I was working hard —and she was supposed to be helping me! Finally I couldn't bear it any longer! I said to Jesus, "Lord, do you not care that my sister has left me to serve alone? Tell her then to help me." *(Suddenly remembers something; her face registers surprise. Puts hand to mouth as if to stop words that have been said.)* Oh! . . . I had forgotten what Jesus said then. . . .

Mary: Martha was very upset with me that time, because I left her with all the serving. She even asked Jesus to make me do my part! I really felt terrible, and I was about to jump to my feet, but Jesus said, "Martha, Martha, you are anxious and troubled about many things; one thing is needful. Mary has chosen the good portion, which shall not be taken away from her." I was just amazed! I was expecting a scolding, and here I was commended! Later I was able to talk to Martha about it. . . .

Martha: After I calmed down and after our guests left, I talked to Mary about Jesus' words: "You are anxious and troubled. . . . One thing is needful. . . . Mary has chosen the good portion. . . ." At first Jesus' words upset me because I couldn't see what he meant. All I could see was my load of work! But later . . . I told Mary that I was sorry I had said those things, and that now I was beginning to understand what had gone wrong. It wasn't so much Mary's problem as it was mine: I have a tendency to worry and fuss about little things, forgetting the truly important ones. Mary tends to concentrate on the important things, leaving everything else behind her. Jesus was teaching about very important things, and there I was bustling around with food. It really wouldn't have made any difference if we had eaten a little later, or if we hadn't had a full meal. Mary chose the good portion, Jesus said. . . .

Mary: My sister is a very strong person. She sometimes tells me that she admires my strength of purpose and what she calls my ability to see the truly important things in life. But if the truth be known, it's Martha who is strong and full of purpose and practicality.

(Pauses, remembering. Sighs, shaking her head.) My brother Lazarus became terribly ill. Martha and I both nursed him, but it was no use. We watched him die right here in this house. We tried to send a message to Jesus, but he was far away, and Lazarus died within a few days of the time we sent the message. I can't remember a time in my life when I felt such despair as I did after Lazarus died. We buried him in a tomb in the hill not too far from here, and then I came home to weep. I was miserable. Even when the word came that Jesus was approaching, I just sat there, unable to respond.

123

Martha: Four days after Lazarus died we heard that Jesus was approaching Bethany. Mary was in deep mourning and I certainly was sad, but as soon as I heard Jesus was coming I ran out of this house to meet him. I may have been the one to fuss about serving and all, but my faith in Jesus was very strong. "Lord," I said to him, "if you had been here, my brother would not have died. And even now I know that whatever you ask from God, God will give you." Perhaps it sounds foolish, but I had such faith in Jesus that even with Lazarus lying in his tomb I felt there was still hope. And Jesus said, "Your brother will rise again." I agreed with Jesus. I said, "I know that he will rise again in the resurrection at the last day." *(Lifts her face up and smiles.)* And then Jesus said, "I am the resurrection and the life; he who believes in me, though he die, yet shall he live, and whoever lives and believes in me shall never die. Do you believe this?"

Mary: My sister told Jesus that she believed he was the Christ, the Son of God, who was coming into the world. . . . Yes, Martha is strong, and she sees and understands *very* well. It was Martha who came to me with the message from Jesus while I was still despairing here in the house. There were quite a number of people here with me, so Martha whispered in my ear, "The Teacher is here and is calling for you."

(Brightens and laughs at herself.) I didn't sit

here any longer! No sooner had Martha given me the message than I ran out of the house and up the road to find him. When I came to Jesus I fell at his feet, weeping again, and I said, "Lord, if you had been here, my brother would not have died." I still was concentrating on what might have been. I missed the hope of what could still be!

Martha: We had never seen Jesus weep, but when Mary came to him in such anguish the tears started falling from his eyes. "Where have you laid him?" Jesus asked. And we all took him to the tomb where Lazarus was buried. A large stone was in place over the entrance to the tomb.

Mary: That stone looked so big and formidable. I took one look at it and started weeping again. My dear brother Lazarus! Inside that place! And Jesus said, "Take away the stone!"

Martha: I said, "Lord, by this time there will be an odor, for he has been dead four days."

Mary: And Jesus replied, "Did I not tell you that if you would believe you would see the glory of God?" . . . And the men pushed the stone away from the tomb. *(Both women are quiet for a moment with stunned expressions on their faces.)*

Martha: First Jesus prayed to his Father in heaven. . . .

Mary: And then Jesus cried out loudly, "Lazarus, come out!" *(Both women sit quietly, stunned.)*

Martha: I could hardly believe my eyes. . . .

Mary: It was unbelievable. . . .

Martha: Our brother Lazarus. . . .

Mary: He came walking out of the tomb, still wrapped in the burial cloths.

Martha: Jesus said, "Unbind him, and let him go."

Mary: We ran to Lazarus, ripped off the cloths so he could breathe freely and move about.

Martha: Lazarus looked as surprised as we felt, but soon he started smiling and he hugged us all. . . .

Mary: Jesus was weeping again, especially when Lazarus threw his arms around him.

Martha: We thanked Jesus over and over. . . .

Mary: And then we took Lazarus home, marveling over the new life given to him.

(The sisters are smiling, remembering. There is a pause.)

Martha: When we heard that *Jesus* had been resurrected, Mary and Lazarus and I all thought of the same thing. . . .

Mary: Lazarus' death and raising to new life was almost like a preview of things to come. Jesus himself died and was in his tomb three days—and then was resurrected! But, of course, the two occurrences were very different, too. Jesus' resurrection sealed his victory over sin and death. Death could not hold the Messiah. It was only through his special intervention that Lazarus was brought back to life. And, of course . . . Lazarus will die again. In fact, there was a time when the Jewish leaders were trying to have Lazarus killed because so many people were following Jesus as a result of the raising. . . .

Martha: But Jesus will live forever in glory! He is our Savior and our Lord. . . .

Mary: Shortly before his death, Jesus visited in our home again. I had some costly ointment which was very fragrant and I anointed his feet with it. The beautiful smell filled the house! And then I wiped his feet with my long hair, because I loved him so much. I meant it all to be an honor for Jesus, a token of my love and faith.

Martha: The disciple Judas criticized Mary for wasting the ointment on Jesus when the money could have been used to help the poor people. But Jesus said, "Let her alone; let her keep it for the day of my burial. The poor you always have with you, but you do not always have me."

Mary: When I thought about it later, I realized that I had not only honored Jesus, but I had anointed his body for burial. Only seven days later Jesus died on the cross. Some of the women came to the tomb early on the day after the Sabbath with their spices and ointments in order to anoint his body —but Jesus was alive! No anointing was necessary!

Martha: Mary honored Jesus with the beautiful ointment while he was yet alive!

Mary: And Martha honored Jesus with her beautiful faith and hospitality!

Martha: Jesus is the resurrection and the life!

Mary: Jesus is our Lord and Savior! (*Both sisters, joyful, exit by their respective doors.*)

Dorcas

Acts 9:36—11:18

Dorcas—DOOR-kus
Joppa—JAW-puh
Rachel—RAY-chul
Delia—DEEL-yuh
Chloe—KLOE-ee
Miriam—MERE-ee-um
Simon—SYE-mun
Gentiles—JEN-tyles
Cornelius—kor-NEEL-yus
Caesarea—seh-suh-REE-ah

Dorcas is a middle-aged woman who carries herself with strength and vitality. She is full of purposefulness and is respected by her friends.

Dorcas is dressed in a fine robe made of linen or wool. She is a wealthy woman who uses her means and talent to help those who are less fortunate.

The scene, the upper room in Dorcas' home, is furnished with a wooden table and at least two wooden benches. An imaginary bed is off to one side. On the table are material, needle, and thread.

An imaginary group of women is gathering to sew for the poor people of their town, Joppa, located by the Mediterranean Sea.

(Dorcas enters, visiting with several imaginary women.) Everyone come in and find a place to sit down! How many do we have today? . . . Five? Wonderful! We have a lot of sewing to do—we can use many hands! *(Picks up her own sewing and sits down.)*

I'm working on some robes for the widow of Jonathan the fisherman. He was lost at sea, remember? . . . Oh, that happened at least a year ago. She has two small children. . . . *(Sews as she speaks.)*

That's true, Rachel. I used to do all the sewing alone. It's been one of the joys of my second life that many of you are willing to share the task!

(Looks around group.) Who is here today? Rachel, Mary, Anna, Delia, Chloe. . . . Where is Miriam? . . . Well? . . . Isn't someone going to tell me about Miriam? Is she sick? What's the matter? Miriam always comes to sew. . . .

(Listens, then registers amazement and disbelief.) She doesn't want to come anymore? . . . I can't *believe* that! It was Miriam who organized this sewing group. Why doesn't she want to come? . . . You needn't look at one another like that. You can tell me whatever it is that's wrong. . . .

(Listens, then nods in understanding, but is unhappy.) Oh. . . . I see. . . . You had a disagreement with Miriam. Well, I know her very well, and I'm sure the disagreement wasn't about Miriam personally. She is the most humble person I know. She must be fighting for someone else. . . .

(Nods as she listens.) *Now* we're getting the whole story. . . . Let's see if I have this straight: Miriam

wanted to invite Susanna, Simon's wife, to be a part of this sewing group. Is that right? . . . Yes. But the rest of you didn't want Susanna in your group. . . . And Miriam is now refusing to come unless you also invite Susanna. I see. Could I ask a very plain and simple question? . . . *Why* do you not wish to have Susanna join this group? She's a very good seamstress and also a very good worker. . . .

(Listens, then puts sewing down in disgust and starts pacing, very upset.) I can't believe what I'm hearing! You're refusing to have Susanna be a part of this group because of her husband's work! Why, Simon the tanner has been in Joppa for many years. . . . Yes, I know that the work of a tanner is considered to be unclean according to oral Jewish law, but, but uncleanness. . . .

(Slowly walks back to her place, picks up sewing, sits down.) My dear friends, we all love Jesus, and we all believe he is our Savior. One of the things Jesus showed us in his life and in his teachings is simply this: Our Lord shows no partiality among people. Remember now . . . remember! Jesus touched people with leprosy and healed them. There is no one more unclean than a leper! And he associated with all sorts of people who were considered unclean and unworthy. And he healed Gentiles as well as Jews. And lately, my friends, the apostles themselves. . . .

(Pauses, trying to decide something, then puts sewing down and speaks very directly to the women.) I have never told anyone about this, but I think it's time everyone knew. Shortly after Peter had prayed for me and God restored my life, a very amazing thing hap-

pened to the apostle. I know this to be true because I was with Peter on the rooftop of Simon the tanner's home when it occurred.

(Stands and moves around in the scene, gesturing for emphasis.) Peter had been staying with Simon and his family. This particular afternoon I was visiting Peter, Simon, and Susanna. After a while, Peter told us that he wished to go on the rooftop to pray and meditate. Later Peter called to me and told me that he would very much appreciate having some food brought to him since he was hungry. So I went downstairs and began to help Susanna prepare the meal. It took perhaps half an hour. Then I carried the food up to the rooftop so Peter could partake of the meal in privacy.

(Pauses, wondering how to explain what she saw.) A very strange thing was happening to Peter. He did not hear me when I told him that the meal was ready. Instead he was staring into the sky with a look of intense concentration. I decided to wait and see if I could help him in any way. I wasn't sure if he was ill or if he was having a vision or if he was just concentrating totally on his prayers. So I sat very quietly and watched. After a few minutes his body started to relax and he rubbed his face and eyes. "Ah, Dorcas," Peter said, "I didn't know you were here."

Peter started walking back and forth on the rooftop. Finally he said, "Dorcas, I've had the most extraordinary experience. I've had a vision: the sky opened, and something that looked like a great sheet descended, let down by the four corners. It came all the way down to earth, right where I was standing. The sheet was full

131

of all sorts of animals, reptiles, and birds. And then a voice said, 'Rise, Peter; kill and eat.' But I refused, saying, 'No, Lord; for I have never eaten anything that is common or unclean.' And then the voice said, 'What God has cleansed, you must not call common.' The voice commanded me to kill and eat three times, and then the whole sheet was taken back into heaven."

I was amazed! Peter was so agitated and excited. He was pacing back and forth, gesturing wildly with his hands, trying to explain the vision to me. He kept saying, "I wonder what it can mean! I *wonder!*"

Well, *I* wasn't much help! I showed him the food and encouraged him to eat, and then felt I should leave him to his own thoughts. No sooner had I come downstairs than we heard voices calling from outside the house. Susanna rushed to open the gate. Three men who were strangers to us asked for Simon called Peter. Just then, Peter himself came down the steps from the rooftop. "I am the one you are looking for; what is the reason for your coming?" Peter asked. And they said, "Cornelius, a centurion, an upright and God-fearing man, who is well-spoken of by the whole Jewish nation, was directed by a holy angel to send for you to come to his house, and to hear what you have to say." And then! Peter invited the men into Simon the tanner's house to be his guests.

(Looks around at the women, nodding.) Yes, you may well gasp! Gentiles in a Jewish home—that's unheard of! Even if the home belongs to an unclean person such as you have called Simon the tanner. But Susanna and Simon were so gracious! They welcomed

the men, offered them food, and provided their best hospitality. In fact, the three men stayed the night in Simon's house!

(Returns to seat and sits down. Picks up sewing but does not work on it.) The next day Peter and the three men and a few people from Joppa, including Simon the tanner, left for Caesarea. Cornelius the centurion lives there.

Well, I won't tell you the whole long story, but the important thing to know is that Peter ministered to these Gentile people in Caesarea and they were baptized in the name of Jesus, and they also received the gift of the Holy Spirit!

(Looks around at friends, nodding.) Yes, it's true. The men from Joppa returned in a few days and told Susanna and me about it. Peter had told them about his vision of the clean and unclean animals, and what he now understood it to mean.

(Pauses, looking around.) What do you think Peter's vision meant? *(Waits, looking at friends.)* Go ahead, Delia, don't be afraid. . . . What do you think it meant? . . . That's right. Our God loves the Gentile people, too, and wants them to have salvation. . . . What else do you think it means? . . .

Anna? . . . What do you think? . . . *(Suddenly smiles and nods vigorously.)* You're right, Anna! You're right! God is teaching us that we are to make no distinctions among people. He loves everyone and he wants us to do the same. God offers salvation through Jesus to *everyone,* and we are to treat all people with love and kindness.

Our Jewish traditions are very deep, and it takes a lot of teaching and persuasion to help us understand that we are to love Gentiles and those we would call "unclean." But regardless of what our traditions say, Jesus taught us to love, and he showed us many examples of such love in his own life. Now the apostles are being shown that our barriers to love are artificial, and they must come down!

(Starts working on sewing. After short pause, innocently looks up and speaks pleasantly.) Now, what was it you were saying about Susannah? . . . *(Smiles and nods.)* Oh, yes, we'll wait. We have all afternoon.

(Returns to sewing, smiling, for a long count of five beats. Then hears someone at door and gets up to greet guests.) Miriam! Susannah! Do come in! I've been waiting for you! . . . We've *all* been waiting for you! . . . Yes, Susannah, of course you may see the bed again.

(Goes to imaginary bed in corner of scene not previously used.) Many people ask to see this bed and to visit this room. This is the bed on which I was laid when I was dead. It sounds so strange to say "I was dead," but you all know it was true. And it was in this room that Peter prayed that I would be restored . . . and I was given a second chance at life.

(Walks to doorway, pauses to look back at friends.) It's a beautiful thing to have a second chance. I have a second chance at life, and we all have been given a second opportunity to live our lives in God's peace and love, without artificial barriers among us.

I've prepared some food, and it's time to serve it. Now *everyone* is here! *(Exits.)*

Mary, mother of Jesus (III)

(In Ephesus, living in John's house)
ACTS 1-4; LUKE 24:36-42

Deborah—DEB-uh-rah
Ephesus—EH-feh-sus
Galilee—GAL-lih-lee
Gentile—JEN-tyle
Magdalene—MAG-duh-leen
Arimathea—air-ih-muh-THEE-ah
Crete—kreet
Mesopotamia—mess-ah-poe-TAY-mee-ah
Aramaic—air-ah-MAY-ick
Samaria—suh-MARE-ee-ah

Mary is an old woman, and she moves slowly
and carefully around the scene. She is wearing a
long dress of a muted color, but not black. She may
be wearing a shawl-like garment to warm her.

A place where Mary can comfortably sit is
required, perhaps a straight chair or a more ornate
wooden chair (not a stuffed chair or rocker). A
bench will suffice if a wooden chair is not available.

Mary is in John's home in Ephesus. Tradition
tells us she died there. She is old, but she is determined and
positive, and her voice is strong.

(Mary enters, moving slowly. She is alone, but soon Deborah, John's teenage daughter, enters to visit with her.)

The storm is beginning. The wind is blowing so hard, and the rain is coming down. The rain will be welcome, I know. The dust on the city streets has been smothering.

(Moves to chair and eases herself into it, relaxing.) I was going to take a walk, but I'll go out when the rain stops. . . .

(Looks toward doorway. Smiles to welcome Deborah.) Deborah! What a nice surprise! Come and visit with me. You can't go back home in the storm—you might as well sit right down here and tell me all about your new husband and your new house! . . .

(Listens, nodding, smiling.) I'm so happy for you, Deborah. You and your fine young husband David will have a wonderful life together. But I do miss having you here at home. Why, I helped you come into this world, my dear. Your mother gave birth to you in this very house 16 years ago, and I washed you and rocked you. Oh, Deborah, you were such a beautiful baby, such a good baby. You've always been a joy to me.

I've lived in your father's house ever since . . . well, ever since my own son died, and it's been wonderful. John and your mother have taken such good care of me—they've really spoiled me, if the truth be known! And I have felt just like a grandmother, watching you and your brothers grow up. But you, Deborah, you have been special. . . . Why? Well, because I was here when you were born, and because you've always loved me and treated me like your real grandmother.

(Smiles, listening.) Well, that is certainly true. Living in Ephesus has separated us from our families in Judea and Galilee, and it has made us a close family, Deborah. The church has grown here, but the fact remains that we are living in Gentile country and that is very foreign to me as an old Jewish woman.

(Looks around, as if she's heard thunder and rain.) Listen to that, Deborah! We're finally going to get the rain we've needed all summer. The thunder is so loud and the rain is pounding on the roof. . . . But I really do like it! It's the sound of new life and growth and potential.

(Listens to Deborah.) Of course you can ask me a question, Deborah. You can ask me anything you wish. . . . No, I don't mind talking about Jesus—I love to talk about Jesus! *(Gets up from chair and walks to side of scene.)* Oh, there was time right after he died that I could hardly bear to speak about him—it all hurt so much. But Deborah—three days after his crucifixion we knew that he had arisen from death and was living again! *(Her voice is strong and joyful.)*

At first I thought someone was playing a cruel trick on me, but soon I believed it was true, especially when I remembered some of Jesus' teachings. And then many of the disciples saw Jesus. . . .

(Returns to chair, but sits on edge as she confides in Deborah.) And, Deborah, *I* saw Jesus, too, after his resurrection! . . . Yes, I really did! You see, there were quite a number of people who gathered together after

137

Jesus died: the disciples, some of the women, including me, and other followers and their families. At first we were just devastated by what had happened on Golgotha hill, but after three days we started hearing reports that he was alive! Peter, John and Mary Magdalene were the first to tell about it, and then Jesus started appearing to the disciples. One evening just shortly after the resurrection we were all together praying in the upper room where Jesus had celebrated the Passover before his death. Suddenly he was there in the midst of us. He just appeared. . . .

Well, all I can tell you is that he was not a spirit—he really was a living person. . . . How do I know? He asked us to touch him, saying that a spirit does not have flesh and bones. And then he asked for something to eat, to prove he was indeed alive. We gave him a piece of broiled fish and he ate it in our presence.

(Gets up and walks about, excited.) Deborah, it was both beautiful and frightening. . . . I had *seen* him die on the cross—I stayed right there until they pierced his side and the blood and water flowed out. There was absolutely no question about it—Jesus was dead. He was buried in Joseph's new tomb, Joseph from Arimathea. . . . Yet, here he was several days later—*alive!* I simply couldn't believe my eyes! But he invited me to touch him, and I did. He was just as real and just as alive as you are, Deborah! . . .

And yet, there was something new about him, too. I recognized him as my son, but now I also recognized him as my Lord and my God. That was the strangest thing of all. And still, it was the most natural thing of all. . . . *(Returns to chair and listens to Deborah.)*

Did I know these things when Jesus was growing up? *(Laughs a little.)* Well, I certainly had a lot of clues. I didn't put them all together at the time, but as I have pondered them over the years, I realize that many things were apparent even then. . . . The angel's words to me were very significant, and words of the prophet at the time of purification in the temple were important. The way Jesus communicated with his Father in heaven, the things he shared with me . . . oh, so many things make sense *now!*

Jesus was on earth for about 40 days after his resurrection, Deborah. During that time I saw him on several occasions. I know the disciples saw him frequently. Your father can tell you about that! . . . And then Jesus ascended into heaven. Your father was on the Mount of Olives with Jesus and the rest of the disciples when that happened, too. After that we didn't see him in the flesh anymore.

(Gets up and walks to doorway, looking out.) Yes, it's still raining—a wonderful, steady rain. The hillsides will be very green again. And we'll see the little flowers appearing!

(Returns slowly to chair; listens to Deborah.) What's that? . . . You want to hear about the special Pentecost day? . . . Oh, Deborah, I've told you that story so many times! And you've heard your father tell about it, too! . . . Well, it's a favorite story of mine, too!

Like I said before, I was with the group of disciples, women, followers, and families that had clustered together in Jerusalem. You have to understand, Deborah, that we were frightened. The authorities had killed Jesus, and we were quite sure they would kill us, too, if they could find us. Rumor had it that I, as Jesus' mother, was a primary target. And, of course, his disciples were badly wanted by the authorities. They were trying to crush this new religion, this new faith. So we were frightened, Deborah, and we hid away from public view.

Before he ascended, Jesus had promised the disciples that he would send his Spirit to come upon them and give them power to be his witnesses. They were to wait in Jerusalem for the coming of the Holy Spirit. *(Pauses, trying to find the best way to explain.)*

Deborah, this afternoon before the storm started, the wind began blowing. Did you hear it? . . . Well, about 10 days after Jesus ascended into heaven, we were all gathered in one of the houses. We had eaten our morning meal together and were praying, when suddenly —we heard the sound of wind blowing through the house, very much like what we heard this afternoon. It was a strong wind and it filled the house. . . . And then we saw something very strange. Little tongues of what looked like fire spread in the room and rested on each one of us. I could see those little flames on everyone else, but at first didn't realize that one was also resting on *me!* . . .

What did it feel like? I never did feel the flame-like tongue, but what I *did* feel was the power of the Holy Spirit. It rushed over me and through me, very much like the wind we were hearing. The experience was incredible, Deborah, and I know I can't explain it to you adequately. Suddenly I was not afraid anymore.

Here we had been hiding away in various houses in Jerusalem, fearing the authorities and what they might do to us—and when we were filled with the Holy Spirit we all poured out of the house and onto the street, telling people about Jesus and how he died, and especially how he had been raised from the dead by God. We had all turned into *witnesses!*

(Listens to Deborah.) Yes, it's true that we all spoke in various languages. That was another power that the Holy Spirit gave us. You see, there were many Jews and Jewish converts from all over the world in Jerusalem right then. They were there to celebrate the harvest festival named Pentecost. These Jews were devout people who wanted to celebrate this festival right in Jerusalem. They were from many different countries, like Egypt, Arabia, Crete, and Mesopotamia. Now, many Jews who had lived in these countries all their lives could not speak Aramaic like we do, and the fact that we could speak in various languages helped us explain the message about Jesus to *everyone,* regardless of where they had come from. . . .

Deborah, when we were able to speak in different languages, it was a symbol of the fact that all barriers among people were to be broken down. The difference in language is one of the biggest barriers there is between two people—you can't communicate with each other. When we could speak the languages of these people, we were suddenly able to communicate very well. The message of Jesus and his resurrection could be spread to *everyone!*

Yes, at first everyone thought we had been drinking a lot of wine very early in the morning. It was only 9:00! But Peter quickly began preaching to the people who had gathered. He explained that God's Spirit had been poured out upon us, and that we certainly had not been drinking wine. Peter preached a marvelous sermon, Deborah. I can still hear the power and assurance with which he spoke! . . . And this was the man who had denied Jesus and who had been cowering in houses with the rest of us!

Three thousand people, Deborah! That was the number of people who received the word of God and were baptized that day. Imagine! . . . Now the authorities could not harm us or harm anyone who believed. in Jesus and his resurrection, because there were so many! We were able to speak very boldly about God and how he had made Jesus Lord and Christ for us. Every day more people believed and were baptized. Soon there were 5000 believers!

Your father and Peter were right in the middle of it, Deborah. There were miracles of healing, there were impromptu sermons in the streets, and soon there were arrests and hearings before Jewish courts. The authorities tried to tell Peter and John not to speak or teach in the name of Jesus, but you can imagine how much good *that* did! Soon the message about Jesus was spreading, not only in Jerusalem, but through Judea and Samaria.

(Gets up and walks around.) I'm an old woman

142

now, Deborah. But, oh, the things I've seen happen in my lifetime! There have been persecutions, of course, but through it all the church has grown and the good news about God's salvation through Jesus has spread through the world. . . . Well! *(Gestures generally.)* Here *we* are in Ephesus! Who would have thought such a thing!

It's very beautiful and precious to me, Deborah, how the word about Jesus continues to be spread, and how the Spirit continues to give power to believers. I'll never forget the despair and the darkness as we stood at the foot of the cross. When I think of it now, I see it as the darkness of sin and evil. But, oh, the joy when we knew Jesus was alive! And I see that as the light and power of God's salvation!

(Goes to doorway and looks out.) Speaking of light and power, have you noticed that the sun is shining? . . . Yes, the rainstorm is over. The dark clouds served their purpose, and now the bright rays of the sun are breaking through.

Come, Deborah, I'll walk with you back to your house. I love to be outdoors right after a rainstorm. The air is so clean and fresh. Did I ever tell you about the storm we had in Nazareth one time? . . . *(Exits through doorway, speaking to Deborah.)*

Lydia

Acts 16:11-40; Letter to the Philippians

Lydia—LIH-dee-ah
Demas—DEE-mus
Claudia—CLAW-dee-ah
Philippi—FILL-ih-pye
Galilee—GAL-lih-lee
Silas—SYE-lus
Drusilla—drew-SIH-lah
Euodia—you-OH-dee-ah
Syntyche—SIN-tih-kih

Lydia is an energetic woman who exudes warmth and enthusiasm. She carries a scroll and occasionally sits on a high stool at the center of the scene.

Lydia wears a long, purple robe, and appears quite well-to-do. She is a successful merchant in purple dye and cloth.

(Lydia is bidding farewell to friends and is eager to read the letter from Paul that arrived during the day.) Goodbye, Demas! Goodbye, Claudia! *(Waves to them at door of her home.)* Have a safe journey! The

light and peace of Jesus be with you! *(Waves again, watching them go. Then closes door and sighs deeply.)*

Finally! I'm alone at last! *(Gazes lovingly at rolled-up scroll she carries.)* We all read this letter from Paul while we were together, but I've been so eager to read it when I'm alone so I can savor every word! It's been so long since we've heard anything from him!

(Settles herself on stool and carefully opens scroll.) "From Paul and Timothy, servants of Christ Jesus, to all God's people living in Philippi who are in union with Christ Jesus, and the church leaders and helpers: May God our Father and the Lord Jesus Christ give you grace and peace." *(Sighs and smiles happily.)* "I thank my God for you every time I think of you; and every time I pray for you all, I pray with joy, because of the way you have helped me in the work of the gospel, from the very first day until now."

(Drops scroll to lap, thinking out loud.) From the very first day, the very first day. . . . Oh, I remember the very first day I heard Paul tell of Jesus! That had to be the crossroads of my life. It was a Sabbath day, and some of us women had gathered on the river bank just outside of Philippi to worship the almighty God, something we had done many times before. It was peaceful and quiet by the river, not like the busy city. We had just sung a psalm, I remember, when we saw several men approaching us. Paul, the leader of the little group, asked if they might join us in worship, and, of course, we said yes! We all sang together and we asked Paul to read the Scripture.

What a strong-looking man he was, not very tall,

145

but just brimming over with vitality and urgency. Something about him compelled me to listen. He read the Scripture, and then he continued talking about it. We heard him talking about the Savior God had sent to earth, Jesus of Nazareth in Galilee of Judea. So far away, and yet here were men traveling for the specific purpose of telling other people about this Jesus.

Oh, my heart burned within me, for we had read many times of the promises God had made to his people—promises about a Messiah who would save us! When Paul, and Silas, too, explained to us that Jesus had died for our sins, and that he had arisen from the dead and ascended into heaven—why, it was perfectly clear to me that Jesus must be God's Son, the Messiah! I begged Paul to baptize me in Jesus' name, and he did, right there in the river! My family was also baptized, along with others from our group. What joy! What joy!

(Picks up scroll and begins reading.) "And so I am sure of this: that God, who began this good work in you, will carry it on until it is finished in the day of Christ Jesus. You are always in my heart! And so it is only right for me to feel this way about you. For you have all shared with me in this privilege that God has given me, both now that I am in prison *(shakes head, sighs)* and also while I was free to defend and firmly establish the gospel. God knows that I tell the truth when I say that my deep feeling for you all comes from the heart of Christ Jesus himself." *(Smiles and nods.)* Yes, I know that.

"This is my prayer for you: I pray that your love

will keep on growing more and more, together with true knowledge and perfect judgment, so that you will be able to choose what is best. Then you will be free from all impurity and blame on the day of Christ. Your lives will be filled with the truly good qualities which Jesus Christ alone can produce, for the glory and praise of God. I want you to know, my friends, that the things that have happened to me have really helped the progress of the gospel. As a result, the whole palace guard and all the others here know that I am in prison because I am a servant of Christ. And my being in prison has given most of the brothers more confidence in the Lord, so that they grow bolder all the time in preaching the message without fear."

(Drops scroll to lap.) Prison. . . . Paul's back in prison again. I wonder how many times it is, now, that he's been imprisoned for the sake of the gospel. And he doesn't seem to mind! He even says it's served to help the cause of Jesus! *(Shakes head.)*

But I think I know what he means. Paul and Silas were in prison right here in Philippi, soon after I had accepted the Baptism of Jesus. Oh, such a ridiculous thing happened! Paul, with the grace of Jesus, had cured a poor young woman of the evil spirit that made her a soothsayer. Poor girl was out of her mind, but the men who controlled her were using her powers to make all kinds of money. And were they *angry* when Paul cured her and she became a normal person again! Not one bit thankful that the girl was well— oh, no! Just furious because their source of income had disappeared.

Those men brought Paul and Silas before the judges in the marketplace, and soon they were being beaten on their bare backs with wooden whips. Finally the judges threw Paul and Silas into prison. The jailer was threatened with his own death if they escaped, so he cautiously placed them in the inner prison and clamped their feet into the stocks. The rest of us came right here to pray and wait. There was nothing we could do except pray, and we did plenty of that!

It was the next day before there was any news, and then it was Paul and Silas themselves who knocked on the door! They had been released and had even received an apology from the judges! It had been discovered that they were Roman citizens and their treatment had been unlawful.

But that wasn't the exciting thing—not really! Paul and Silas told us that they had been praying and singing hymns in the prison when suddenly, about midnight, a strong earthquake loosened the chains of all the prisoners and threw the prison doors open! We felt the quake here in my house, too. The poor jailer was so sure that the important prisoners had escaped that he would have killed himself, but Paul and Silas stopped him in time. The jailer was so astonished to find them still in the prison that he begged to hear more about this Jesus that they had been praying to and singing about. And so it was that the jailer and his entire family heard the good news, and they all were baptized. The jailer washed the wounds on Paul and Silas' backs and even fed them a wonderful meal. Paul said it was a joyful household!

(Picks up scroll and searches for a particular place.) Let's see, where was that statement I wanted to read again. . . . Here it is: "Does your life in Christ make you strong? Does his love comfort you? Do you have fellowship with the Spirit? Do you feel kindness and compassion for one another? I urge you, then, make me completely happy by having the same thoughts, sharing the same love, and being one in soul and mind. Don't do anything from selfish ambition or from a cheap desire to boast; but be humble toward each other, never thinking you are better than others. And look out for each other's interest, not just for your own."

(Drops scroll to her lap.) That's a sin I have to watch out for all the time, and I think Paul knows it. It's so easy, being in business the way I am, to think only of myself and my business interests. Before I knew Jesus I didn't think twice about overcharging a little, or measuring cloth a little short. I'm one of the few dealers in purple dye and purple cloth, so people need my goods. I didn't think it would hurt business to cheat a little, putting some extra money into the business. But knowing Jesus has changed all that for me. Suddenly I knew it was wrong to shortchange anyone or to cheat people of their rightful property. Satan likes to tempt me with an opportunity to do just that once in a while, but I struggle hard against it. That's not Jesus' way.

(Picks up scroll, searches for a place.) I'll read some of this later. It was toward the end of the scroll that there was something I wanted to read tonight. . . . "So then, my brothers—and how dear you are to me, and

how I miss you! How happy you make me, and how proud I am of you!—this, dear brothers, is how you should stand firm in your life in the Lord. Euodia and Syntyche, please, I beg you, try to agree as sisters in the Lord." *(Impatient and exasperated.)* Maybe those two will quit quarreling if *Paul* tells them to! . . . "And you, too, my faithful partner, I want you to help these women, for they have worked hard with me to spread the gospel, together with Clement and all my other fellow workers, whose names are in God's book of the living. May you always be joyful in your life in the Lord. I say it again: Rejoice!" That sounds just like Paul! Rejoice—be joyful!

(Reads again.) "Show a gentle attitude toward all. The Lord is coming soon. Don't worry about anything, but in all your prayers ask God for what you need, always asking him with a thankful heart. And God's peace, which is far beyond human understanding, will keep your hearts and minds safe, in union with Christ Jesus."

There Paul sits in prison, and he tells *us* not to worry! Well, if that's *his* attitude, the least *we* can do is imitate it!

"In conclusion, my brothers, fill your minds with those things that are good and deserve praise: things that are true, noble, right, pure, lovely, and honorable. Put into practice what you learned and received from me, both from my words and from my deeds. And the God who gives us peace will be with you." *(Closes scroll, gets down from stool.)*

Peace . . . joy . . . those are the stamps of a Christian.

Oh, how we needed to hear that again! I'm so happy this letter arrived from Paul. I can only have it tonight, and then I must pass it on to Clement so everyone can have a turn reading it. But for tonight it's mine! I wish I could memorize every word!

(Starts to pray; may drop to knees or simply raise head.)

Oh, God, thank you for this letter! You have answered our prayers in sending it. You knew how much we needed to hear these words from Paul. Lord, I thank you for Paul and Silas, Timothy, and Luke! And I thank you for all the Christians right here in Philippi. Most of all, Lord, I thank you for making me one of your own. May your peace and the joy of Jesus surge into my very being. In the holy name of Jesus I pray. Amen . . . and so be it. *(Exits, holding scroll close to her heart.)*

Priscilla

Acts 18:1-21; Romans 8:1-4; 16:3-5

Aquila—uh-KILL-ah
Tullius—TOOL-yus
Ephesus—EH-feh-sus
Gentiles—JEN-tyles
Damascus—duh-MASK-us
Ananias—an-uh-NYE-us

Priscilla is a mature woman with strength and energy. She is dressed in a long gown of ordinary color and fabric—a working dress.

The time is middle afternoon. The location is Priscilla and Aquila's home in Ephesus in Asia Minor.

A high stool may be in the scene, for Priscilla to occasionally rest on as she speaks.

(Priscilla enters, carrying on a conversation with a scribe, a young man who will write down her dictated letter.)

Come along, Jason, come right in here. . . . You can sit on this bench *(gestures to imaginary bench)* while you write the letter I'm going to dictate.

I'm sorry to hear that Mark is ill. He's been scribe to Aquila and me for about a year now. I do hope the illness is not serious. . . . Well, that's good. When you see Mark, be sure to give him our good wishes for an early recovery.

In the meantime, Jason, I'm happy you could fill in for Mark, and I do appreciate your coming on such short notice. I'm anxious to send this letter off yet today. Tullius leaves for Athens tonight, and he has promised to take the letter to my sister if it's ready by nightfall.

Well, are you ready, Jason? . . . Write this.

(Speaks carefully, rather slowly. Moves about scene, gesturing, occasionally resting on stool.) To my sister Joanna, living in Athens, from her loving sister Priscilla in Ephesus. . . . I was overjoyed to receive your letter, and especially to hear the good news of the birth of another nephew! Aquila and I welcome little Benjamin into the family. He is joining a wonderful mother and father and a beautiful group of brothers and sisters. We hope and pray that we will soon meet little Benjamin in person.

(Pauses, pondering her next words carefully.) My dear Joanna . . . I feel the need to answer some of your questions about my work and about my Christian faith. . . . You are already familiar with how Aquila and I became Christians in Corinth, and how our friend Paul taught us about Jesus and the salvation God has given us through him. Praise be to God! . . . We have been in Ephesus two years, teaching many people about

this same Jesus and being messengers for God in this large and busy city.

(Paces, anxious about how to make herself understood. Pauses to think about her words.) In your letter you remind me of our Jewish heritage and our Jewish faith and upbringing. You ask if I have forgotten my Jewish faith, and you plead with me to return to the tradition of the family. . . . My dear sister, how I wish I could speak to you in person. I am afraid that my love and my joy in Jesus will not be conveyed to you adequately by means of a parchment letter. If only I could *show* you and *share* with you personally the love of Jesus Christ!

(Pauses to think about words.) Joanna, please listen to me. I have not forgotten my Jewish heritage or my Jewish faith. On the contrary, my Jewish faith is the bedrock of my Christian faith! . . . Surely you remember the many times we heard the words of the prophets read to us. Remember how our dear father would say, "Some day, my daughters, some day the Messiah will come."

Joanna, my beloved sister, I believe Jesus is the Jewish Messiah. He is the fulfillment of the law and the prophets. How I wish father were alive so he could know that the Messiah has finally come! . . . I have not given up my Jewish faith, Joanna. Instead, I have been given the beautiful gift of the *completion* of my Jewish faith! Jesus is the beginning and the end, the alpha and the omega. How I wish you could know Jesus as I do!

(Alternately paces and sits on high stool, concentrat-

154

ing on her words, choosing them carefully.) Do you remember how we have worried about keeping the Jewish law perfectly? Do you remember how our mother taught us the laws and regulations about the preparation of food, and how our father taught us the laws about the Sabbath, and tithes, alms, and prayers, and all the laws for daily living? We tried so hard to keep all the laws because we believed that God looked with favor on us only if we kept the law. . . .

Joanna, we knew then and we know now that we did not keep the law perfectly. It just isn't possible. And for Jewish people that is very bad news, because it means we're condemned by God—we have not kept the law no matter how hard we've tried and how many sacrifices we've made. The law showed us what sin was, but it could not make us righteous and without sin.

(Goes to imaginary bench where Jason sits.) Jason, read those last few lines back to me, will you? *(Assumes a listening stance, waits a few moments, then starts pacing again.)*

Thank you. . . . *(Dictates again.)* But, Joanna, the good news for Jewish people is that God knows our pitiful condition and he has provided a way to perfectly keep the law! . . . No, it's not through our efforts, nor through the sacrifices made to atone for the sins. The way God makes us perfect and righteous is through his Son, Jesus Christ! Jesus paid the price for all our sins and our sinfulness in his once-and-for-all sacrifice on the cross! And then he rose from the dead, establishing victory over death!

Just think, Joanna! You don't have to worry about how many steps you take on a Sabbath, or how much dill and cumin to use in cooking. In Jesus we know that those regulations are superficial, and that the important thing is our relationships to God and to other people. And you can receive forgiveness through Jesus Christ for those sins of envy and pride and impatience and taking God's name in vain—God is ready to forgive us through Jesus! God loved you and me and all people so much that he sent Jesus to be our Savior, to save us from our sins, something the law could not do.

Paul's teachings about Jesus have helped me so much, Joanna. I've heard him say this: "There is therefore now no condemnation for those who are in Christ Jesus. For the law of the Spirit of life in Christ Jesus has set me free from the law of sin and death. For God has done what the law, weakened by the flesh, could not do: Sending his own Son in the likeness of sinful flesh and for sin, he condemned sin in the flesh, in order that the just requirement of the law might be fulfilled in us, who walk not according to the flesh but according to the Spirit." The Spirit, Joanna, is God's presence within us. It is a beautiful and bountiful gift sent to us for strength and power after Jesus ascended into heaven to be with his Father.

(Pauses, sighs sadly.) It is true, of course, that many Jewish people do not accept Jesus as the Messiah, as the Savior, as the fulfillment of the law and the prophets. It makes me so sad, Joanna, because I believe Jesus is the completion of our Jewish faith. What

he taught and how God used his life here on earth makes sense in such a deep and profound way when a person has experienced the Jewish faith and teachings. There are times when I really feel sorry for the Gentiles because they haven't had the rich foundation and preparation that we Jewish people have had!

Yes, as you stated in your letter, I spend quite a bit of time with Gentiles. I know that Jews often will not have dealings with Gentiles, according to the law and traditions, but that is different now, too, Joanna. The Gentiles need to hear the message of love and salvation through Jesus Christ just as much as the Jewish people do. Paul describes himself as an apostle to the Gentiles, even though he, too, is Jewish.

Paul says Jesus himself appeared to him in a vision on the road to Damascus when Paul was persecuting the Christians, and his whole life was changed. An old disciple in Damascus named Ananias told Paul that the Lord had revealed to him that Paul should carry the good news of Jesus before the Gentiles and kings and the sons of Israel. Aquila and I are results of Paul's ministry in Corinth. And we, in turn, tell the good news about Jesus here in Ephesus to both Jews and Gentiles! It's often hard, Joanna, but God's Spirit strengthens us and protects us.

(Pauses to think.) My scribe Jason is nearly to the end of the parchment, and his fingers grow weary. This letter will reach you by the hand of Tullius, a fellow Christian here in Ephesus. Aquila greets you. We send you and your husband Joel and your children our love. We pray for you daily.

(Moves to imaginary bench where Jason is sitting.)
Now, Jason, let me sign my name at the bottom of that parchment. *(Goes through motions of signing name.)* There! The letter is finished, and it does look very nice. You did a fine piece of work, Jason! Now, if you'll roll the letter up tightly and wrap it in a piece of animal skin, it can be delivered to Tullius. . . .

(Acts as if listening to scribe.) Yes, I did say that the Gentile people are included in the message of salvation in Jesus. . . . You felt you could not come to Jesus because you're a Gentile? Oh, Jason, Jesus died for the sins of *all* people, Jews and Gentiles alike. All he asks is that we let him do his saving work in our lives—that we accept him as our Savior. . . . Yes, it's true, my young friend Jason!

(Walking toward exit, continues to speak to Jason.) Well, I'm glad you were the scribe today, too. I thought I was only speaking to my sister, but it's turned out that I was also speaking to you! . . . Tell you what, Jason, after you've delivered that letter to Tullius, come back here and share the evening meal with Aquila and me. We'll tell you all about Jesus! That's a story we love to tell! *(Exits.)*

Bibliography

Although the dramas incorporate imaginary thoughts and actions of biblical women, the basis for these thoughts and actions is in the Bible. I have used the following books to aid me in depicting the dramatic moments in the lives of these women.

Black, Matthew, general editor. *Peake's Commentary on the Bible*. London: Thomas Nelson and Sons, 1962.

Deen, Edith. *All of the Women of the Bible*. New York: Harper and Brothers, 1955.

Deen, Edith. *The Bible's Legacy for Womanhood*. Old Tappen, N.J.: Fleming H. Revell, 1969.

Herr, Ethel. *Chosen Women of the Bible*. Chicago: Moody, 1976.

The Interpreter's Dictionary of the Bible. New York: Abingdon, 1962.

Wight, Fred H. *Manners and Customs of Bible Lands*. Chicago: Moody, 1953.